It's Okay to Not Like Cauliflower

Finding Freedom in Living Your Authentic Self

Dr. Bobbi Avery

Published by Avery Publishing

First paperback edition, 2026

Library of Congress Control Number: 2026903031

ISBN: 979-8-9946722-0-4

This book is a work of nonfiction. The experiences, observations, and reflections expressed are those of the author and are drawn from real-world leadership and professional contexts. To protect privacy and confidentiality, identifying details, names, and characteristics of individuals, organizations, and institutions have been changed or omitted, and in some instances composite examples are used.

This book is intended for informational and reflective purposes only and does not constitute medical, psychological, or mental health advice, diagnosis, or treatment. Readers are encouraged to seek the guidance of qualified professionals regarding their individual circumstances.

Printed in the United States of America

Table of Contents

Author's Note

This book reflects my personal experiences, insights, and lessons learned throughout my leadership practice. The perspectives shared here are rooted in lived experience, self-reflection, discomfort, and growth.

What you will find in these pages is not empirical research, nor a prescriptive formula for leadership. It is a collection of truths shaped by the paths I have walked, the mistakes I have made, and the wisdom I continue to seek.

I invite you to engage with this book through your own lens. Take what resonates, question what challenges you, and leave behind what does not serve you. This is not a roadmap. It is an invitation to explore your leadership identity and self-limiting beliefs with curiosity, courage, and care.

Preface

There comes a moment when we realize we have been trying too hard, not in a way that builds strength or character, but in a way that quietly unravels the self. We pursue careers that no longer speak to us. We hold on to relationships that erode our peace. We find ourselves in situations, conversations, and expectations that require us to shrink, twist, or mute our true nature to belong. We nod when we want to resist. We endure when we are meant to evolve.

This book is born from a persistent tension between who I am, who I have been expected to be, and who I am becoming. It explores the cost of that misalignment, the exhaustion that comes from constant performance, and the disservice we do to ourselves and others when we live by force instead of flow. We all carry internal struggles related to leadership. I wonder if some of mine are familiar to you.

This is not a story of rebellion. It is a story of returning. Returning to myself, to my truth, and to the inner knowing that is often drowned out by internal and external expectations and the pressure to perform.

It's Okay to Not Like Cauliflower is both a guide and a companion. It reminds us that conflict does not always threaten harmony. Sometimes, it clears the air and deepens understanding. But this book is not only about navigating friction with others. It is also about the grace we extend to ourselves when we recognize that something, or someone, no longer supports who we are becoming. There is freedom in letting go of what we have carried out of obligation, and power in forgiving ourselves for waiting so long to set it down.

When I talk about "performing," I am describing the version of myself I present when I believe it is what others expect. It is the polished, agreeable self that avoids conflict and rejection. It is the careful mask I wear when I edit my truth to match what I think others want to see or hear. Over time, this performance erodes clarity, diminishes contribution, and pulls me further from my sense of self.

Through reflection, I continue to ask myself where I learned to perform in the first place. What societal messages shaped these expectations? What pressures did I internalize and then work tirelessly to unlearn? The danger of performance is that it teaches us our worth depends on meeting external demands, even when those demands do not align with who we are.

Left unchecked, it can leave us uncertain of what we believe or need, simply because we have spent so long trying to be what others expect.

Performing as a leader became my default, often without my awareness. It did not happen all at once. It was a quiet accumulation. A compromise here. A silence there. A nod when I wanted to question. A smile when I wanted to pause. I believed I was doing what good leaders do: adapting, accommodating, and meeting expectations. Somewhere along the way, I lost parts of myself.

Today, my leadership practice is grounded in the intentional creation of psychological safety. I believe deeply that when people feel accepted for who they are, they can participate more fully, honestly, and courageously. I continue to ask why this kind of safety is so difficult to sustain in workplaces, and what it requires of leaders who are willing to examine themselves.

At its core, this book explores leadership identity, and the role participation plays in shaping it. Leadership is not a title, but a way of showing up as a whole person: present, aligned, and engaged. Participation begins with self-reflection. It asks us to lead from personal values, to hold space for accountability, and to remain aware of the influence we carry. It is not about control or perfection. It is about self-awareness.

Participation invites us to look inward before acting outward, to lead with honesty even when it feels uncomfortable, and to remain curious about the impact we create. True participation is presence with purpose. It is how leadership becomes human, vulnerable, and transformative.

Although this book is rooted in the workplace, authenticity is not limited to professional settings. You bring your full self into every room you enter, whether it is the boardroom, your home, or the quiet moments within your own mind. Leadership identity is not only about how you lead others. It is also about how you lead yourself. The way you show up for yourself will always shape how you show up for others.

Let this be your invitation to reconnect with the parts of yourself that have been silenced, reshaped, or hidden in the pursuit of performance. This is your opportunity to pause, reflect, and rediscover who you are and how you choose to lead, not only at work, but in every space you occupy. Let this be the beginning of leading from wholeness, honesty, courage, and care.

Let's begin.

With authenticity, curiosity, and love,
Bobbi

Introduction

Leadership is never just about strategy or results. It has always been about people, presence, the choices we make, and the truths we carry.

This book was written to explore a different kind of leadership, one that begins not with performance or perfection, but with authenticity, self-awareness, and participation.

In a world that often values appearances, many of us have learned to perform. We have internalized the idea that success requires us to be composed, agreeable, and endlessly motivated. We reshape ourselves to meet expectations that do not reflect who we truly are. Over time, that disconnect erodes our well-being and distorts our leadership identity. The cost of belonging in ways that betray ourselves eventually becomes too high. And yet, we stay. Until something inside us realizes we can no longer ignore the tension between who we are and who we have been pretending to be.

This book is a call to reconnect with yourself. It reflects on what it means to lead with honesty, wholeness, and courage. Each chapter examines aspects of leadership identity often overlooked in traditional models, including emotional discomfort, self-awareness, generational differences, impact, and personal legacy. These are not just ideas. They are daily practices. They are choices made in quiet moments of reflection, discomfort, and sometimes reckoning.

As you read, you will be invited to examine the stories you have believed about leadership and yourself. You will be encouraged to sit with discomfort, not as something to fix, but as something to understand. You will have space to ask difficult questions and find clarity in the answers that emerge.

This is not a book of formulas. It is a framework for building your leadership compass, grounded in your values, your truth, and your vision for how you choose to show up in the world. Whether you are a new leader finding your voice or a seasoned leader seeking to rediscover it, these pages offer space to reflect, realign, and recommit to leading with intention.

You will not be told what type of leader to be. Instead, you will be asked who you are when you are no longer performing and who you are when you are fully present.

Because that is where the most powerful kind of leadership begins.

This book is for the person ready to embrace it all, the good, the uncomfortable, and the parts of themselves they have worked hard to hide, deny, or outrun. It is for the leader who seeks more than titles and results. It is for the individual who wants to feel aligned, not just productive. It is for those tired of performing and curious about what it might be like to lead as themselves.

It is for those of us who have fallen into the trap of contortion, who have performed their way into leadership roles only to realize they feel more disconnected than ever, and who quietly wonder whether success is possible without constantly editing themselves to meet someone else's standards.

It is for the person who has remained silent when they wanted to speak, who has shape shifted to fit into rooms where they never quite belonged, and who has made themselves smaller in the name of keeping the peace or climbing the ladder. It is for those beginning to wonder what it might look like to stop conforming and start connecting to themselves, to their values, and to the people they serve.

This book is also for those who feel called to lead differently. For those willing to examine their identity, challenge their patterns, and commit to leadership that values integrity over appearances. It is for those who want to lead from the heart and be remembered not just for their accomplishments, but for the integrity they uphold in every decision, conversation, and connection.

If you are an emerging leader looking to develop your leadership compass, this book is for you. Leadership is not defined by title alone. It is something you cultivate with intention and purpose. This work invites you to shape your leadership identity through participation, authenticity, and self-reflection, offering a starting point for defining what you stand for and how you choose to lead.

It is also for the person living in quiet denial, the one who tells themselves they are good enough not because they truly believe it, but because admitting otherwise feels too heavy to face. It is for the leader who has convinced themselves that performance is enough, that titles, accomplishments, and constant motion somehow compensate for the disconnection they can no longer ignore.

This book is for the person who senses, even faintly, that something is missing. For the one who wonders in quiet moments whether they have settled for a version of leadership that looks right on the outside but feels empty inside. It is for anyone who has achieved success by every external standard, yet still carries a deep, persistent question. Is this all there is.

If that is you, if you have ever felt the tension between who you are and who you pretend to be, this book is your permission to stop pretending that it is enough. Not because you are insufficient, but because you deserve something more genuine, more connected, and more aligned. This is your invitation to move from settling for good enough to being fully engaged, fully present, and entirely yourself.

Whether you are a seasoned executive, a new manager, or someone navigating the quiet tension between who you are and who you have been expected to be, this book offers you space. Space to reflect, realign, and reconnect with yourself. The most powerful kind of leadership begins not with performance, but with participation. And not with perfection, but with permission.

I hope the experiences shared in this book offer you the jump start I never had, the clarity I had to find through trial, error, and the discomfort of unlearning. Let these insights serve as guideposts as you build your own leadership compass with greater confidence and intention.

I encourage you to read each chapter slowly and with care. Pause when something stirs. Reflect deeply. The goal is not to rush to the end, but to grow with honest intention, especially in moments when you notice an emotional shift.

This book is grounded in love and humanity, written with the hope that you will recognize pieces of yourself in its pages and remember that you are never alone in the work of becoming.

Welcome to the work.
Welcome to the return.

Chapter 1
Cauliflower Crusted
The Veneer of Performance Over the Substance of Participation

I spent most of my adult life trying to like cauliflower. It sounds silly when I say it out loud, but it’s true. I roasted it, riced it, blended it, smothered it with sauces and spices, even buried it under mountains of cheese. I tried every trick because cauliflower was a superfood, sneaking into pizza crusts and mashed potatoes, praised by every health blog and wellness guru. It wasn’t just a vegetable anymore. It had become a symbol, a marker of discipline, of health, of doing life the "right" way. Everyone else seemed to love it. So why didn’t I? Each bite felt like a test I kept failing. I seasoned it differently. I reminded myself it was good for me. I told myself it was harmless, and that I should like it. I kept trying to make myself like something that just wasn’t for me.

Until one day, sitting at my kitchen table and pushing aside yet another forkful of mashed cauliflower on my plate, I finally admitted what I had been avoiding for years: It’s okay to not like cauliflower. It was a moment of sharp clarity, undeniable and charged with the weight of everything I had been forcing. I had spent so long trying to convince myself to accept what my palate could not, believing something must be wrong with me because I didn't feel what everyone else seemed to. But the truth was simpler. I didn't like cauliflower, and that was okay.

What surprised me wasn't the confession itself but the sense of relief. There's a specific kind of tension that builds up when you spend years struggling with yourself, trying to shape a version of you that was never meant to fit. You learn to distrust your instincts. You become skilled at silence. You convince yourself that with just a little more effort and a bit more discipline, you can bridge the gap between who you are and who you think you should be.

Eventually, you begin to think that the problem is you, a flaw or deficiency you haven't fixed yet. So, when the truth finally emerges, even as a quiet acknowledgment of what has always been, it feels less like liberation and more like surrender. But it's not. It's freedom.

It's the feeling of releasing a burden you didn't know you were carrying. The first full breath after years of shallow ones. The moment you realize the chains were never locked. You were just holding on too tightly.

We have learned that humans are wired for belonging and conformity. We are shaped by millennia of staying close to those who knew us, our circle, our people, as a matter of survival. When we feel out of sync with our preferences, instincts, or when our feelings don't match the group, it causes deep discomfort. The mind tries to fix this, often by blaming ourselves. You don't just think, *"I don't like this."* You think, *"There must be something wrong with me."* So, you try harder. You eat the cauliflower. You laugh at the joke. You pretend to enjoy the meeting. You wear a mask, nod along even when you disagree, stay silent when a colleague crosses a boundary, or adopt team habits, even unhealthy ones, to avoid standing out.

This pressure is especially strong in environments lacking psychological safety, where dissent is punished or discouraged, or where power dynamics are steep. Employees may hide their true thoughts, change their behavior, or compromise their personal values to "fit in." Over time, this kind of conformity can cause emotional exhaustion, resentment, and a loss of authentic voice. High performers may shrink to stay palatable. Innovation stalls. Biases remain unchallenged. And the workplace becomes a space of performance, not genuine participation.

The Weight of Performance

There is a distinct difference between performing and participating. Performance is usually driven by the desire to meet expectations, gain acceptance, and preserve social harmony or personal reputation. It involves aligning words, actions, and body language that are considered appropriate or favorable in a particular situation. The aim is often to avoid conflict, minimize risks, or earn approval from others.

While performance often emphasizes appearances, it also seeks to keep interactions safe and predictable. Performance is driven by the desire to fit in, meet expectations, and avoid saying or doing anything that might break the established norms. When employees feel they must perform rather than be their authentic selves, the culture shifts from one of contribution to one of survival. People start to carefully control their every move, choosing words that sound agreeable rather than honest, nodding in meetings even when they disagree, and working overtime not out of passion but out of fear of being seen as replaceable. The focus shifts from innovation to managing impressions. Authentic voices are silenced not because they lack value, but because the environment signals that safety lies in sameness. In a performance-driven culture, vulnerability is often mistaken for weakness, and curiosity is undervalued unless it receives approval from senior leadership. People begin to withhold their best ideas and most creative solutions because they are busy reading the room rather than changing it. Collaboration becomes superficial. Decisions are made to avoid conflict rather than foster growth. Initiative is replaced by compliance, and feedback becomes a feared exchange rather than a shared opportunity for growth.

Living this way is exhausting. It's confusing. It separates you into two: the real you and the person you show to others. And this act isn't accidental. It's intentional. It's fueled by a deep, often unspoken instinct for survival. We perform because, at some point, it became necessary.

We perform to protect our jobs because organizations often reward conformity over authenticity. We try to preserve fragile relationships, whether romantic, professional, or social, by believing that shrinking ourselves is better than risking disconnection. We aim to maintain our place in communities, political climates, with colleagues, boardrooms, marriages, and friendships, carefully reading the room and adjusting our approach accordingly. At first, it seems wise. Necessary. Sometimes, it even feels noble: sacrificing a little of yourself for the greater good. But over time, the cost can become devastating.

I know this firsthand.

For years, I convinced myself that leadership meant giving everything I had. Six days a week, fourteen-hour days, I wore exhaustion like a badge of honor. I believed that sacrifice proved my worth, that the more I gave, the more I belonged. But slowly, the cost started to show. My body gave the first warning signs, then my emotions followed. I was tired in ways that sleep could not fix. The things and people I loved most outside of work started to fade into the background. And somewhere along the way, my spirit dimmed.

Still, I kept going, believing that the crushing workload was the price of significance. I had a close relationship with a person who was at the center of decision-making, someone I deeply respected. So, when I finally found the courage to voice my frustration and share how it was affecting me, I expected understanding, maybe even support. Instead, I was met with a response that respected the system more than the person: "We didn't ask you to work this way." And at that moment, I felt like the floor dropped out from under me. I felt betrayed. Invisible. Unappreciated. Everything I had sacrificed, everything I thought I was proving, felt erased by that one sentence.

It took me a long time and a lot of honest reflection to see the deeper truth: they were right. *They hadn't asked me to work that way.* I had placed that expectation on myself. I had built my identity around a distorted definition of value, one that equates exhaustion with importance and martyrdom with worth. In trying so hard to perform, to prove, to earn my place, I became my own worst enemy. No one demanded the impossible from me, but I did.

This is one of the most painful, humbling lessons about performance: sometimes, the pressure doesn't come from outside. Sometimes, it comes from within. We internalize others' expectations and magnify them until they become our own self-imposed cages. We believe that love must be earned, that belonging must be bought, and that leadership must be proven through self-erasure. However, real value and true leadership do not require self-destruction. They do not demand you sacrifice your well-being on the altar of others' perceptions. Performance might secure a seat at the table, but authenticity allows you to survive and thrive there. The moment you stop performing is the moment you start reclaiming yourself. It's the moment you realize your worth was never meant to be measured in hours worked, sacrifices made, or exhaustion endured.

It's not an easy realization. It's painful. It's complicated. But it's also profoundly freeing.

Once you recognize the trap, you can start the slow, courageous process of stepping out of it. You can redefine your values, not based on performance but on presence. Not based on exhaustion but on integrity. Not based on sacrifice but on sustainability. You can choose to lead yourself first. In doing so, you become the leader and the person you were always meant to be. The moment you allow yourself to tell the truth, *such as "I don't like this*," you reclaim your agency. You reclaim your wholeness. You no longer live in two realities. You live in one.

The relief is profound because it signals the end of the deafening conflict inside you. The pressure lifts. The self-doubt quiets. The permission to simply be arrives like a quiet exhale, refreshing what has long been held tight. And maybe the most beautiful part of it? It doesn't just free you in that one area. It spreads outward, easing every part where you've been forcing yourself to conform. It teaches you to ask: *What else am I holding onto that I can finally put down?* That's when the real work and true liberation begin.

Cost of Leadership Performance

When leaders choose to lead through performance instead of participation, they inevitably silence the perspectives and lived realities of others. This is a costly failure of responsibility and respect. These leaders may cling to control, achieve success, and maintain appearances, but the organization will be limited in its ability to grow. It's important to recognize that a performing organization can still meet conventional standards of success. Revenue targets might be reached, operations could run smoothly, and teams may appear aligned on the surface. However, success based solely on performance is inherently limited. It might deliver quick wins or impressive outputs, but it reflects lack of optimization and can be unsustainable. This kind of success is fragile, collapsing when circumstances change or challenges demand responses beyond metric-focused approaches. Over time, the constant pressure to perform fosters exhaustion and burnout, draining the energy and creativity organizations need to thrive and be optimized.

Performance-driven cultures can hinder innovation. When individuals are evaluated only on their ability to achieve expected results, they become less willing to take risks or challenge the status quo, behaviors that are vital for producing breakthrough ideas. This environment fosters superficial relationships, where trust remains fragile and conversations stay at a surface level, preventing teams from gaining the psychological safety necessary for genuine collaboration and growth.

When I discuss psychological safety, I mean a space where employees feel comfortable and are encouraged to share their perspectives and experiences related to business practices openly. It is an environment built on trust that leadership will listen with curiosity and respect. Defensiveness is absent, intimidation is outdated, and emotional reactivity is not present.

This is where leaders gain true insights into what employees are thinking, feeling, and experiencing. However, make no mistake, building psychological safety requires effort. It demands discipline to listen actively, seek understanding, and release the need to control. Leaders must resist the impulse to defend and instead engage in honest dialogue.

When leaders commit to this practice, they unlock the greatest opportunity available to them. It is the chance to build a culture rooted in collaboration, trust, and mutual respect. It is in this space that organizations move beyond performative success and begin to optimize their full potential. Real success is not about appearances or polished metrics; it is about the collective energy of people who feel seen, supported, and inspired to contribute. That is the kind of success that endures.

Leadership based on performance often creates dangerous blind spots. Blind spots form when leaders become so focused on outcomes, image, or efficiency that they lose sight of their leadership impact. These leaders may believe they are motivating or inspiring others yet unintentionally silencing them. When the drive to *appear effective* outweighs the desire to *be self-aware*, presence becomes performance, and people around them start to shrink.

Blind spots may appear as a lack of awareness, but they are rooted in unexamined influence. They appear when a leader stops asking, *how does my energy, tone, or decision-making shape the space I'm in?* Without reflection, power goes unchecked, and empathy gets replaced with judgement.

Blind spots suppress dissenting voices and ignore diverse perspectives, which reinforces biases and hampers the organization's ability to adapt to evolving dynamics. As a result, organizations that operate this way often face a gap between their stated values and the actual experiences of their people, gradually eroding their culture from the inside out. I want to repeat this again. As a result, organizations that operate this way often face a gap between their stated values and the actual experiences of their people, gradually eroding their culture from the inside out.

True awareness requires leaders to pause long enough to see what their own behavior stirs in others, not through defensiveness, but through curiosity. It's the difference between saying, *"I lead people,"* and asking, *"How do people experience my leadership?"*

Leadership based on denial and vertical thinking creates a perfect recipe for missing opportunities. When people are afraid to speak honestly or question decisions, valuable insights go unspoken and are lost. Ideas that could spark innovation or solve ongoing issues never reach the table. Risks that might lead to breakthroughs are avoided to maintain safety and appearance. In a performance-driven culture, growth is limited not by a lack of skill but by invisible barriers created by fear, denial, conformity, and unspoken truths.

If you are a leader who often dismisses or challenges your employees' perspectives and lived experiences, and if your first reaction is emotional defensiveness rather than curiosity, it indicates a need for self-reflection. This behavior not only damages relationships but also limits growth, innovation, and trust within your organization. When employees feel their experiences are ignored or invalidated, they learn that their voices don't matter. Over time, this creates a culture of silence, where valuable insights are withheld and key opportunities for improvement are missed. The potential for creativity, problem-solving, and genuine engagement is hindered in environments where only the leader's perspective feels safe to express.

The Power of Alignment

Alignment is the essence of organizational optimization. It is the invisible thread that ties people, purpose, and participation together. It is not about repeating the mission statement or posting the company values on the wall. Alignment shows up in the small, often unnoticed choices: how we handle pressure, how we treat others when there is nothing to gain, and how we lead when it would be easier not to.

But let's be honest, alignment runs much deeper than that. It is when an employee's personal values actually connect with the organization's values. It is that quiet harmony you can feel when people are satisfied, proud, and genuinely happy to be part of something that reflects who they are. You can hear it in their tone, see it in how they show up, and sense it in the energy they bring to their work. That is alignment.

And here is the truth many leaders do not want to face: alignment does not happen by accident. It happens because leaders create it. It is built through relationships, through knowing your people beyond their job titles, and through communicating with intention, not performance. If you do not take the time to understand who you work with, what drives them, and what matters to them, you are leading in isolation. You may think things are fine, but that is not alignment, it is avoidance.

Alignment is a mirror. It reflects how deeply your team trusts you, how safe they feel to be honest, and how much of themselves they are willing to bring forward. If you are not seeing that, it is not a team problem, it is a leadership problem.

Alignment is the engine of organizational health and performance. Without it, even the most talented teams eventually stall. When employees feel disconnected from their company's values or unsafe to bring their full selves to work, they start showing up smaller. They give less, not out of rebellion, but out of self-protection.

When people walk through the door and feel they can be who they truly are, their honest, imperfect, human selves, they move differently. They think more creatively, connect more deeply, and give more freely.

That kind of energy cannot be forced. It is earned through respect, appreciation, and the celebration of authenticity and vulnerability.

Many leaders miss this truth. Alignment is not measured by a mission statement on the wall or the results of an engagement survey. True alignment is reflected in employee retention, in trust, and in the energy you feel when you walk into a room. When people stay, when they grow with the organization, not just in it, that is the clearest indicator of a culture where alignment is alive and well.

As a leader, you subscribe to one of two belief systems. You are either content with the success you already have, or you are fully committed to exploring all that is being left on the table. The first mindset relies on control, metrics, and what is easily measured. The second requires courage because it asks you to look beyond performance and into people.

That is where many leaders fall short. Looking into people is messy. It requires patience, vulnerability, and the willingness to hold space for what is real, fear, uncertainty, conflict, and emotion. It means being brave enough to ask uncomfortable questions and strong enough to listen to the answers. That kind of leadership does not always feel efficient, but it is the kind that transforms.

Leaders who choose to keep it safe, who cling to predictability or distance themselves from discomfort, are also choosing to leave brilliant potential on the table. For leaders who focus only on maximizing the bottom line, the untapped potential within people is the bottom line. That is where innovation, loyalty, and profit live. Ignoring that is more than a missed opportunity; it is complacency disguised as success.

Make no mistake, organizations can be successful even if they never fully optimize their people's potential. But that success comes at a cost. They leave behind a wealth of missed profit, creativity, and possibility by failing to put into practice a leadership commitment to employee participation. True participation cannot be mandated; it has to be invited. And it begins with one simple promise, that employees can participate without fear. When people know they can speak honestly, share ideas, and show up fully, the organization does not just grow, it flourishes.

When alignment is missing, you can feel it in the culture long before you see it on a balance sheet. It shows up in quiet quitting, the silent withdrawal of effort and passion. Employees do what is required but no more. They disengage from innovation, stop offering ideas, and begin to emotionally detach from their teams and customers. Clients feel it when enthusiasm fades and relationships become transactional. Turnover rises, taking knowledge, trust, and morale with it. Every resignation costs more than recruiting and training; it erodes consistency, damages reputation, and weakens culture. The cost of disengagement is not just financial, it is the slow decline of creativity, collaboration, and pride. When people stop caring, the organization stops evolving.

As leaders, when you notice a shift in enthusiasm, do not look away. Do not convince yourself it is just a phase or someone else's responsibility to fix. A decline in energy is rarely about disengagement; it is often a quiet signal of disconnection. Pay attention to it. Lean in with empathy, not judgment. Leadership carries the responsibility to ensure employees feel supported, seen, and valued. It is not enough to hear them; you must validate their experiences. When employees know their emotions are met with understanding rather than criticism, trust begins to rebuild. They stop protecting themselves and start participating again. Alignment is restored when people feel safe to show up as themselves and believe their leaders are right there with them, not above them. That is how cultures heal, and how organizational health truly takes root.

Alignment and participation are often treated as metrics to be validated through surveys and scorecards. Numbers might tell a story, but they rarely tell the truth about culture. The truth lives in what you see and hear every day, in how teams talk to one another, how freely ideas move across levels, and how people describe their work in the moments that feel unfiltered. It is revealed in the consistency of behavior when leaders are not present, and in the sense of belonging you can feel the moment you walk into a space. It shows up in the way people protect the culture, the way they celebrate others' wins, and the way they respond when mistakes happen. These are the signals that prove whether your organization is optimized or simply operational. The data is in the behavior, not the survey.

Alignment requires courage. It challenges leaders to see the whole person, not just the performance. It is where leadership evolves from managing outcomes to cultivating potential. It is where optimization becomes more than a goal, it becomes a living reflection of people thriving together. When employees feel safe to be real, they stop performing for approval and start participating from purpose. That is when organizations do not just operate, they come alive.

The Courage to Participate

In contrast, participation driven organization creates conditions where opportunities can be fully realized. When leaders actively invite and reward diverse perspectives, they unlock the creative potential within their teams.

Participation fosters a culture where people are encouraged to contribute unique insights and are recognized for doing so. It is an environment where difference is not just tolerated but celebrated. Diverse experiences and viewpoints are considered essential assets, not threats. This openness enhances the organization's ability to innovate, adapt, and grow beyond what performance alone can accomplish.

An organization can succeed through performance, but it thrives through participation. The difference lies not only in results but also in the sustainability of those results and the level of engagement from contributors. Deep engagement means more than just superficial involvement or passive agreement. It reflects a culture where employees are not only encouraged but also expected to participate in meaningful problem-solving, challenge assumptions, and actively help shape the organization's future. Without active employee involvement in addressing challenges and co-creating solutions, the organization risks operating with a limited viewpoint and leaving untapped potential behind. Participation deepens commitment, boosts collective intelligence, and ensures that growth is not only achieved but also maintained.

When people are engaged at this level, they provide insights, innovations, and solutions that leaders alone cannot see. Leaders must understand that the most significant breakthroughs will never come from the top alone. They will emerge from the collective brilliance of those empowered to participate, question, and create. If you are not making space for this, you are leading blindly. This isn't just a strategic advantage; it is essential for unlocking the full potential of an organization.

Too often, we confuse leadership with performance. Leadership is never about control; it's about connection. It is never about perfection; it's about presence. But presence requires something many leaders avoid: vulnerability.

Vulnerability is not a sign of weakness; it is the clearest proof of our humanity. It shows that we experience emotions, have doubts, and feel the burden of our decisions, just like everyone else. In leadership, vulnerability sets apart those who lead from those who truly embody leadership. It opens the door to trust, strengthens relationships, and encourages the psychological safety needed for people to show up fully, sharing ideas, questions, challenges, and more.

This opens up a level of opportunity that performance-based leadership can never achieve. It is the kind of opportunity that transforms not only processes or products but also relationships, mindsets, and the very identity of the organization itself. New solutions emerge because more voices are encouraged to contribute. Better decisions are made because leaders are willing to acknowledge their blind spots. The organization becomes more agile, more resilient, and more deeply connected to the people it serves.

At this level, opportunity isn't measured solely by revenue or market share, but by the organization's ability to adapt, influence, and sustain its success through collective intelligence and shared ownership. This is where true organizational greatness resides, not in polished performance, but in the brave, messy, and transformative efforts of genuine participation leadership.

True participation begins with clear personal values. It means knowing what you stand for and what you're unwilling to compromise. Values shouldn't remain just abstract ideas or occasional thoughts. They must guide your decisions, influence your actions, and shape how you interact with others. Leading with this honesty makes it easier to be fully present and participate confidently. People notice when your actions align with your values, and this consistency builds trust, strengthens relationships, and fosters meaningful contributions.

And even with clear values, participation does not happen in a vacuum.

When personal values align with the environment's values, participation feels natural, energizing, and sustainable. The trouble begins when we ignore the misalignment. When we feel the disconnect but continue to perform anyway, we silence what feels off. We justify what we know is wrong. We stay in systems that do not reflect who we are or what we believe.

This isn't sustainable. Forcing ourselves to accept conditions that conflict with our values gradually erodes our sense of agency. Nodding in agreement while feeling internal grief causes a slow drift from our core beliefs. Over time, we might forget what we truly stand for. That is the quiet heartbreak of choosing performance over participation.

We owe it to ourselves and those around us to address that misalignment as soon as we notice it. Take a moment to ask, "Is this environment aligned with who I am?" "Do I believe in what I'm contributing to?" "Is this performance, or am I truly participating?" Reconciliation can lead to honest conversations, a change in role, a redefinition of purpose, or even a brave departure. Reconciliation will always bring clarity.

And with clarity comes freedom, the freedom to choose how we show up and to re-enter our lives from a place of truth. Participation isn't a luxury; it's the foundation for longevity in both career and self.

Organizations become sustainable when their members are not just performing roles but engaging with heart and honesty. This occurs when there's alignment between personal and organizational values; when employees and leaders feel empowered to bring their full selves to the table. When there's misalignment, or when we force ourselves to stay in environments that contradict who we are, something begins to break. We lose touch with our inner compass, going through the motions while gradually disconnecting from what once mattered.

The invitation is this: pay attention. If you find yourself forcing what no longer fits, pause. Ask what your discomfort is trying to tell you. It may be time to realign. It may be time to stop performing and start participating. This is difficult work. But it is essential because the quality of our leadership depends on the quality of our self-awareness. Our ability to lead others with honesty and care begins with our willingness to lead ourselves with integrity and grace. Leadership is never about control. It is about connection. It is never about perfection. It is about presence. True leadership starts with the courage to look inward, reflect deeply, and build the compass that guides you with integrity and purpose.

Chapter 2
The Cauliflower Conundrum
Why You Won't Like Everyone and How to Lead Anyway

It took me years to realize that cauliflower wasn't the only thing I had been forcing, it showed up in leadership, friendship, and family too. I kept running into the same quiet self-doubt every time I didn't naturally connect with someone: a colleague who drained my energy, a team member who tested my patience, a co-worker who left me feeling heavy after every conversation, or a family dynamic that required more effort than ease. Instead of accepting what was true, I turned the discomfort inward. I mistook easy chemistry for good leadership, and when it wasn't there, I felt a quiet sense of failure because I couldn't always create relationships that felt mutually sustaining. It wasn't that I believed I had to like everyone. I simply hadn't yet learned how to lead well while accepting that not every connection is meant to be reciprocal.

For leaders, self-doubt often is not about believing we are incapable. It is about believing we should be able to make every relationship work smoothly and naturally if we are doing our jobs well. When that doesn't happen, we often conclude quietly and unfairly that we lack some fundamental leadership skills rather than recognizing the complexity of human dynamics.

Here's a truth I wish someone told me sooner: you don't have to like everyone you lead. Respect is essential. Fairness is non-negotiable. Empathy is critical. But liking? That's optional. No one mentions that. Instead, we're taught to smooth over differences, to put on smiles despite disconnection, to treat diplomacy as an endless cycle of suppressing resentment. But that approach, while polite, is incredibly draining. It erodes authenticity. It damages trust, not just with others, but within yourself as well.

What if leadership didn't require sameness or easy chemistry to be effective? It might look like this in practice. You lead someone you do not naturally click with. Your styles are different, your instincts often misalign, and conversations take more effort than ease. Still, you are clear with one another. You name expectations. You give direct feedback. You stay curious rather than critical. You do not force warmth that isn't there, and you do not pretend the relationship is something it is not.

Instead, shift your perspective and hold this truth:
We are different. Understanding is not guaranteed. Commitment is.

Leadership does not require compatibility to be effective, nor agreement to be respectful. It requires consistency, intention, and the courage to remain clear when relationships are complex. No forced smiles. No pretend friendships. Only clarity, respect, and truth. This is what leadership looks like when it is rooted in integrity.

Some of the most challenging people you encounter, the ones you don't naturally click with, might end up growing the most under your guidance. And if you let them, they might challenge you in ways that contribute to your growth. This is where the work deepens. Because learning to lead people you don't naturally connect with often brings you in direct contact with your own resistance, and yourself.

The Moment of Resistance

The growth that changes us most usually begins with discomfort. Not the kind of growth that comes from achievement or external validation, but the kind that reshapes how you see yourself and the world around you. Sometimes it's a complicated conversation, a moment of unexpected feedback, or a perspective that feels uncomfortable at first. But if you stay open, if you resist the urge to defend or retreat, you'll often find something valuable on the other side. That value, however, is often wrapped in vulnerability. Feedback has a way of landing directly on our most sensitive places, the spaces where effort, identity, and expectation collide. And it is in those moments when feedback strikes a nerve, that the real work of leadership begins.

Those moments ask for something different from us.

When someone offers feedback that unsettles me, the instinct to defend, explain, or retreat can be immediate. Instead of reacting, I begin by taking a deep breath. That small pause creates space between what I feel and what I say and often interrupts the urge to protect myself. I ground myself by remembering that discomfort does not equal danger and that I can feel unsettled and still remain present and safe.

I listen carefully to what is being said, not to prepare a response, but to understand the message. I let the other person finish. As I listen, I pay close attention to what emotionally triggers me. I make a mental note of the moment my body tightens or my thoughts rush ahead, knowing I will want to return to that reaction later. For me, those triggers are rarely accidents. They usually signal a place where I have work to do, where my approach or perspective in building relationships may need refinement.

In the moment, I resist the urge to argue, correct, or explain myself. I do not need to agree right away. I acknowledge that I have heard the feedback and commit to reflecting on it. I thank the person for sharing their perspective, recognizing that honest feedback requires courage, even when it arrives unexpectedly.

Later, in a quieter space, I return to the conversation. I reflect without an audience and with curiosity rather than judgment. I revisit the trigger I noticed and ask what it might be teaching me. Often, it points directly to the very place I need to lean in, the place where growth is asking for my attention. From there, I choose one thing to carry forward into my leadership practice. Growth does not require total agreement. Sometimes it begins with a single, uncomfortable truth.

Be grateful for the opportunity to grow in ways that comfort and affirmation alone would never allow. This is how we move from self-doubt to self-trust, not by avoiding discomfort, but by staying with it long enough to learn.

Learning to stay with discomfort changes how you relate not only to feedback, but to yourself. Over time, you begin to notice how often self-doubt has been less about the situation in front of you and more about the expectations you carry into it. Letting go of those expectations creates room for a quieter kind of clarity, one that does not require you to fix or force what was never meant to be easy.

When you stop trying to season the cauliflower just right, hoping this time it will taste different. It won't. And that's okay. The bigger lesson beneath it all is this: give yourself grace. You are not broken because you don't like everyone. You are not failing because you don't feel an effortless bond. You are human. And leadership was never about perfection or chemistry. Leadership has always been about truth and presence. Not just the kind of truth we speak aloud, but the kind we carry in quiet consistency of who we are.

Leadership is not just a role. It is a practice of self-acknowledgment. A commitment to self-discovery. It begins not with the authority to lead others, but with the courage to face ourselves honestly.

Authentic Leadership involves showing up with honesty, compassion, and grace, even when it feels uncomfortable or uncertain. Performance relies on control and predictability. In contrast, participation requires presence. It asks us to engage purposefully, reflect on our values, and lead with integrity. Participation is rooted in connection, with ourselves, our teams, and the shared values of the organization. Growth isn't always loud or dramatic; sometimes it arrives quietly. It sneaks in through small moments that challenge us to go beyond habit, to reflect on why we do what we do, and to grow in unexpected ways. It's in those quiet moments that the most meaningful leadership begins.

When Self Doubt Shows Up

Self-doubt is sneaky. It shows up when the stories we carry, stories about endless patience, universal likability, and perfect connection, clash with reality. Self-doubt tells us we're not enough. But self-doubt is not guidance. Self-doubt is not leadership. Self-doubt is not truth. Self-doubt tends to sneak in when we face uncomfortable truths, like realizing we don't like someone we work with or that a role we've committed to no longer feels right. In a perfect world, we'd accept these feelings as normal, human responses. But in the workplace, where professionalism is often tied to constant harmony, disliking a colleague or questioning your enthusiasm for a task can seem like a personal failure. Self-doubt can whisper that we're being unfair, unkind, or ungrateful. It urges us to suppress feelings, smile through discomfort, and just keep going.

When this self-doubt goes unexamined, it can lead to emotional exhaustion. We overcompensate by taking on more work, avoid honest conversations, or pretend everything is fine to quiet internal conflict. We suppress frustration to maintain team morale or downplay our needs to avoid being seen as difficult. However, this kind of suppression doesn't promote collaboration; instead, it breeds resentment. It disconnects us from our integrity and makes authenticity feel risky.

Emotional exhaustion is more than just feeling tired; it's a deep, ongoing depletion that affects your energy, motivation, and sense of self. It often develops gradually and quietly, until even simple tasks feel overwhelming. At work, it can seem like dragging yourself through the day, dreading meetings you once enjoyed, or struggling to focus on tasks that used to come easily. You might feel irritable or numb, become quick to snap, or shut down quickly. Things that once sparked curiosity now seem like burdens.

Emotionally drained individuals often describe moving through their days on autopilot, functioning but detached from the experience. An inner voice repeats, *just get through the day*, accompanied by quiet self-doubt about not doing or being more. Over time, emotional exhaustion erodes confidence, dulls creativity, and takes a measurable toll on both physical and mental health.

Perhaps the most painful part of emotional exhaustion is feeling isolated. You might start to pull away from coworkers, avoid social situations, or feel like no one truly notices how hard you're trying. When exhaustion stems from unspoken conflict, unrealistic expectations, or a lack of psychological safety, it becomes even more challenging to recognize and address. Recognizing it is the first step, not as a sign of weakness, but as an indication that something needs attention, adjustment, or release. The truth is, we're allowed to not click with everyone. We're allowed to outgrow people, roles, processes, or even values that once suited us. The goal isn't to eliminate these feelings but to acknowledge them without shame and respond with clarity and compassion, rather than self-doubt. When we do this, we create space for honest conversations, clearer boundaries, and more sustainable work engagement. Letting go of self-doubt doesn't mean abandoning professionalism; it means leading from a place of self-awareness and emotional maturity.

I spent decades trying to like cauliflower because I thought I was supposed to. It was widely praised, promoted, and presented as the right choice. So, I seasoned it and tried to hide it, hoping I'd someday enjoy the taste. I spent decades doing the same with people, convincing myself I had to get along with everyone and manufacture a sense of connection and ease in every relationship. I believed that being worthy of belonging meant always making room for connection, even when it felt forced or fake. I thought it meant ignoring my instincts, pretending the bond was real when it wasn't, and carrying the weight of that disconnect in silence. I hid my dislike with over-accommodation, suppressed my instincts to be polite, and confused forced harmony with emotional maturity.

Now I understand better. I no longer force what doesn't feel true. I have learned that liking everyone isn't necessary to show respect, and that respect doesn't mean I have to abandon my boundaries. I can accept differences without pretending they don't exist. I show respect where I can't feel affection. I offer fairness where chemistry falls short.

And most importantly, I lead with honesty rather than self-doubt. Self-doubt made me perform, adjusting myself to fit what I thought leadership required. Honesty allows me to be clear, direct, and consistent, even when connection does not come easily. That consistency, between what I say, what I do, and what

I expect, is what I mean by leading with integrity. That integrity allows me to handle tension with grace rather than avoidance. It reminds me that leadership isn't about being liked by everyone; it's about being trustworthy, clear, and consistent, even when it's difficult, especially when it's difficult.

When I sit across from someone I don't naturally connect with, I don't panic anymore. I don't tense up trying to find the right smile or scramble for common ground. I don't rush to fix the discomfort or silence it with false enthusiasm. And most importantly, I don't layer self-doubt on top of it like I used to. I used to believe that disliking someone, even if it was gentle or silent, was a personal failure. I thought it meant I wasn't empathetic enough, open enough, or evolved enough. So, I would overcompensate. I would nod more, offer more, and agree more, all to override what I felt.

But now, I understand better. Now, when that familiar discomfort arises, I allow it to be there without shame. I recognize it and support it. And in that quiet moment, I often reflect on a surprisingly pivotal life experience: sitting with a forkful of mashed cauliflower I had tried so hard to love. I recall the relief that washed over me when I finally whispered the truth to myself: *I don't like this. And that's okay.* That small moment turned into a larger permission. It gave me the words to name an even more profound truth: *It's OK not to like cauliflower. It's okay not to like everyone.*

What I have learned, and what I hold onto fiercely, is this: it is never okay to stop leading with integrity. Discomfort is not an excuse for disrespect, and lack of chemistry is not a reason to abandon professionalism. I can honor my truth while still treating others with fairness, dignity, and care. I can coexist with differences without trying to erase it. That is leadership for me. Not forcing connection, not performing harmony, but staying grounded in honesty while upholding respect. Integrity lives in the space between authenticity and compassion. It is truth delivered with care, boundaries without punishment, and honesty that remains accountable for its impact. In that space, we do not say everything we feel, but we do not pretend either. We choose clarity over comfort and respect over approval. And when we do, leadership stops being about being liked and becomes anchored in trust.

Chapter 3
Know Your Cauliflower
Understanding the Types of Difficult People in Your Life and Why It Matters

Before we explore strategies for growth, peace, and success, let's have an honest talk about cauliflower. Not the vegetable, of course, but the people in your life who feel like emotional cauliflower: hard to digest, sometimes bitter, and oddly persistent no matter how many times you try to push them to the side of your plate. These individuals are tough, draining, and often disrupt your emotional and mental clarity.

Everyone encounters a cauliflower or two in their lifetime. The work is not in pretending they do not exist, but in learning to recognize them, understand their impact, and respond with intention and self-compassion. This chapter is not about labeling people as villains. It is about protecting your emotional ecosystem so you can live and lead with clarity rather than depletion.

You cannot fix what you don't first acknowledge. Failing to identify the difficult people in your life allows them to quietly influence your mood, energy, and even your decision-making. Difficult people can consume emotional bandwidth, distort your sense of self-worth, and increase your stress levels, all without you consciously realizing what's happening. This isn't just about annoyance or conflict; it's about protecting your emotional reserves. If left unaddressed, chronic exposure to difficult people can disrupt your mental health, compromise your physical well-being (hello, stress-related illnesses), and derail your professional and personal goals. Identifying your 'cauliflower' is not an act of judgment; it's an act of self-preservation.

In both our professional and personal lives, balance is not a luxury; it is a necessity. Emotional overload caused by difficult people often leads to burnout, conflict, disengagement, or poor decision-making. When boundaries are repeatedly tested or violated, you stop operating intentionally and begin reacting instead.

This kind of balance isn't about managing time or simply learning to say "no." It's about managing energy. Who receives your time, attention, patience, and empathy matters. Knowing who drains you (your cauliflower) allows you to recalibrate and direct your energy toward what truly matters: joy, connection, creativity, and impact.

Work relationships can be some of the most psychologically demanding because we don't always get to choose who we interact with. In the workplace, difficult people can significantly affect your ability to participate and feel appreciated. You might find yourself working harder than necessary, trying to keep the peace, or putting in extra effort to compensate for someone else's poor behavior. The stress can be overwhelming, and the toll it takes on your mental and physical health can be greater than you realize.

Consider, for example, the person who subtly undermines your efforts. This individual pretends to offer "help" or "feedback," but they consistently find ways to weaken your contributions. They are the ones who make passive-aggressive comments, send your work back with cryptic suggestions, or publicly correct you in a way that makes you doubt your abilities. In my experience the underlying psychology usually stems from insecurity or envy. They are motivated by the need to feel superior or validated, and in their attempt to elevate themselves, they end up tearing you down. The result is self-doubt and anxiety, along with the familiar surge of impostor syndrome that often appears just as you are on the verge of succeeding.

Then there's the credit taker, the person who benefits from your hard work without contributing equally. They might pass off your ideas as their own, steal your spotlight, or pretend to be the mastermind behind the success. This individual is motivated by the need for validation or status, and the effects on you include frustration, resentment, and eventually a deep sense of cynicism. Over time, you might lose the motivation to give your best because your contributions are constantly being stolen.

Another common cauliflower in the workplace is the constant critic. This individual approaches nearly everything with skepticism, rarely satisfied and always scanning for flaws. What presents as high standards is often a need for control, expressed through relentless nitpicking that leaves you feeling as though nothing you offer is ever quite enough. Over time, this posture of skepticism and critique can freeze your participation and erode your confidence, leaving you second-guessing every move.

Then, there's the drama magnet. For them, every issue turns into a crisis. They operate in a constant state of emotional chaos, and you inevitably get caught up in it. Whether it's an overblown personal drama or a minor work hiccup blown out of proportion, the energy they bring is exhausting. Often, this behavior stems from emotional dysregulation or unresolved personal trauma and leads to emotional fatigue for those around them. The impact on you is distraction, disengagement, and a growing sense of resentment.

And then, there's the boundary bulldozer. This person disrespects your time, personal space, and emotional limits. They text you at all hours, ask for favors beyond your capacity, or show up uninvited, assuming you'll always make time for them. Their sense of entitlement or lack of boundaries can leave you feeling exhausted, resentful, and out of balance in your work and personal life. When your boundaries are repeatedly ignored, you lose the ability to recharge and protect your emotional well-being.

In many workplaces, we tend to focus on obvious conflicts like raised voices, direct confrontations, and policy violations. However, some of the most damaging dynamics come from what's harder to notice: calculated silence, passive exclusion, and performative smiles. They glare when you speak in meetings. They smirk with quiet disdain, seemingly amused by your efforts to participate, their expressions speaking louder than words ever could. Sometimes, they smile with manic intensity that feels less friendly and more controlling. In group conversations, they intentionally exclude you, avoiding cyc contact, never directing comments your way, making you feel invisible. In the hallways, they pass by without acknowledgment or give only the most minimal, performative nod. This isn't overt conflict; it's quiet dismissal that gradually erodes your confidence and sense of belonging. These behaviors might not violate company policy, but they breach something deeper: the culture of trust and inclusion that healthy organizations rely on. When someone consistently excludes a colleague through body language, dismissive glances, or subtle social maneuvers, it sends a powerful message: this is about control, an intentional power play designed to make you feel small and remind you that belonging isn't automatically granted; it's withheld. Often, it's carried out by someone who never raises their voice or breaks a rule, making it even more insidious. Because the behavior is so subtle, it's difficult to identify and even harder to confront without feeling like you're overreacting. But the impact is real, it's a form of emotional erosion.

This type of emotional tension worsens toxicity because it not only affects the targeted individual but also shapes the environment for everyone. Others begin to pick up on cues, whether they realize it or not. Some imitate the behavior to stay in line with power, while others withdraw, fearing they'll be next. Over time, this creates a culture of caution instead of collaboration. Innovation slows down, psychological safety drops, and trust becomes scarce. People start to perform rather than participate, stay silent instead of share ideas, and prioritize self-preservation over collective progress. Sometimes, it doesn't take a full conflict to poison a culture; all it takes is one person quietly weaponizing social cues. If left unaddressed, the cost goes beyond personal issues to organizational health. The workplace then becomes a place where people just get by rather than thrive.

In your personal life, the stakes are often even higher because these individuals have more direct emotional access. Whether they're family members, partners, or close friends, their influence can be overwhelming and deeply harmful if not managed properly. The blurred lines of love, history, or obligation can make it difficult to enforce boundaries and create the emotional distance needed for self-preservation.

Consider the spotlight stealer as an example. This individual makes every conversation about themselves, showing little empathy for your feelings or experiences. They make you feel small when you're vulnerable, and their constant need for attention can drain you emotionally. At their core, the spotlight stealer often faces deep insecurity, but their grandiosity hides it. For you, the effects include ongoing self-blame, low self-esteem, and emotional confusion. You might find yourself questioning your worth or apologizing for things that aren't your fault.

Then, there's the over giver. This person constantly sacrifices their time and energy but always ensures you're aware of their selflessness. They thrive on guilt, using it as a tool to manipulate your emotions and decisions. Their victim mindset and fear of rejection create a cycle of emotional manipulation and codependency, where you're repeatedly drawn into their drama and made to feel responsible for their happiness.

The enabler is another type of difficult person who can quietly disrupt your personal and professional life. They defend or justify others' bad behavior, often causing you to doubt your own perceptions. In the workplace, this can look like tolerating an employee's repeated disrespect, missed deadlines, or boundary violations because addressing it feels too risky. You tell yourself it's not worth the conflict, that they're too valuable to lose, or that calling it out will only make things worse. Over time, this avoidance reinforces the behavior and leaves you carrying the emotional weight of a problem that isn't yours to solve alone.

Whether it's a partner who ignores your needs or a family member who shields a loved one from the consequences of their actions, the pattern is the same. Fear of conflict or abandonment keeps the behavior intact, trapping you in a cycle of frustration and helplessness. The impact on you includes suppressed emotions, chronic frustration, and a growing sense that you can't trust your instincts.

Some difficult people in your personal life include relatives or friends who overstep boundaries. These are individuals who think they know what's best for you and become overly involved in your decisions. Whether they give unsolicited advice or try to push their plans onto you, their need to control can make you feel like you've lost your independence. It's emotionally exhausting and undermines your sense of autonomy and self-reliance.

The silent punisher is another sneaky presence. This person may punish, confuse, or manipulate by withdrawing emotionally or refusing to communicate. They make you chase their approval or attention, causing you to second-guess every interaction. Their fear of vulnerability or need for control through detachment can create an environment filled with anxiety and emotional disconnection, leaving you constantly on edge.

At their core, most difficult people act from unmet needs such as control, validation, power, attention, or safety. While this doesn't excuse their behavior, understanding their motives helps you depersonalize their actions. Not every conflict is about you; often, it reflects their inner chaos. However, being empathetic doesn't mean being a doormat. You can care deeply and still maintain strong boundaries. You can understand and still say "no." True emotional peace starts with that clarity.

Chronic exposure to difficult people triggers the body's stress response. Your brain perceives threats, even emotional ones, and releases cortisol and adrenaline. Over time, this may cause insomnia, digestive issues, brain fog, fatigue, depression, anxiety, and a weakened immune system. You cannot achieve high performance or inner peace while silently absorbing the toxicity of difficult relationships. Recognizing and managing these relationships is not a luxury; it's a health necessity.

Here's where intention turns into action. Your goal is to name your cauliflower, recognize the triggers they activate, and create emotional distance, whether through boundaries, communication, or exit. Start by listing your cauliflowers: write down the people who leave you feeling depleted, anxious, small, or unseen. Next, identify your triggers: what do they do that triggers your emotional response? Is it the tone, how they show up, or the lack of recognition? Once you spot the pattern, define your boundaries, what you will no longer tolerate, engage with, or be available for. Then, create emotional space. Sometimes this means physical distance, but other times it involves reframing how much power you give their behavior. Finally, seek support, therapy, coaching, or trusted friends, to help you stay accountable to your peace. You can't control the cauliflower, but you can control your plate. Knowing who your cauliflower is helps you understand your emotional environment and take deliberate steps to protect your energy.

We often concentrate on identifying difficult people in our lives, but there's another crucial step we tend to overlook; recognizing ourselves as part of the problem. This doesn't mean blaming ourselves for everything that goes wrong, but it does mean understanding that sometimes we contribute to our own suffering, often without realizing it. At the core of this is the ego, the part of us that craves validation, approval, or love. This aspect of ourselves often causes us to tolerate disrespectful or hurtful behavior because we believe we can change the other person or because we secretly hope that, if we endure enough, they'll finally recognize their faults and apologize. The truth, however, is that people change when they want to, not because we wish them to. And the longer we stay, hoping for a transformation that never happens, the more we damage our own emotional and physical well-being.

At its core, the ego doesn't just crave validation; it thrives on it. In relationships, whether personal or professional, we often remain in unhealthy dynamics because we believe we can "fix" the situation. There's a deep-seated need to feel *needed*, to be the caretaker, the fixer, the person who is indispensable. This is especially true when we feel insecure or fear that our value is tied to our ability to serve others. But this need to be needed often causes us to tolerate toxic behavior to prove our worth, often to our own harm. The longer we tolerate it, the more we become stuck in unhealthy patterns, leaving us emotionally drained and confused.

Similarly, there's a strong desire to be liked and appreciated. In both work and personal relationships, we often tolerate disrespect or mistreatment because we don't want to be seen as "difficult" or "high maintenance." We fear that speaking up will lead to rejection or conflict, so we endure the bad behavior, silently hoping that if we wait long enough, the other person will change. This pattern is especially common in relationships where we feel a deep need to be desired, whether by a partner or a colleague. We may stay in unhealthy dynamics, convinced that if we prove our loyalty or affection, the other person will eventually recognize our worth and change. But this belief is a trap. The truth is, change doesn't come from our endurance; it comes from the other person's self-awareness and willingness to grow. Our efforts to fix things or win their approval are often misguided and only prolong the cycle of disappointment.

What keeps us stuck in these situations is a complex psychological mix of fear and attachment. Fear of loss, in particular, plays a significant role. Humans naturally dislike uncertainty, and the unknown is often more frightening than the pain of staying in a situation that no longer benefits us. The thought of walking away from a relationship, job, or lifestyle, no matter how unhealthy it is, can seem terrifying. The familiar discomfort appears less daunting than the uncertainty of what might come next. As a result, we hold on to what we know, even if it's harming us. This fear of loss is often paired with a subtle but widespread belief that we still have control over the outcome. We tell ourselves that by staying and enduring, we can direct the situation toward a better result, but this is just an illusion. We can't control other people's actions, and trying to do so only leads to more frustration and pain.

This attachment to unhealthy situations often causes delays in taking action. We stay in jobs that drain us, relationships that aren't reciprocal, and friendships that have long outlived their usefulness because we believe we're still handling the situation, or that somehow, if we wait long enough, things will magically get better. But in reality, this prolonged attachment only wears us down. Our emotional resources become depleted, leaving us feeling exhausted, resentful, and disillusioned. The toll this takes on our health is staggering. Constant exposure to toxic situations isn't just mentally exhausting; it can also manifest physically. Stress, emotional strain, and the anxiety of waiting for change wreak havoc on our bodies. Sleep problems, digestive issues, tension headaches, and even more serious long-term health problems like hypertension or weakened immunity can result from remaining stuck in these harmful dynamics.

And then there's the subtle, insidious effect of losing ourselves in the process. When we stay in an unhealthy relationship or job for too long, we often forget who we are outside of the conflict. Our sense of self becomes buried under layers of other people's drama, manipulation, or neglect. We stop listening to our own needs and desires because we're so focused on managing someone else's behavior. Over time, this leads to feelings of emotional numbness or even a loss of identity. We've sacrificed so much for the sake of others that we forget what it feels like to nurture our well-being. This dynamic is difficult to break, but the first step is recognizing it. Acknowledging that we might be part of our suffering is uncomfortable, but also very empowering. It means we can change. We don't have to wait for others to change their behavior or for life to suddenly improve. We can choose to walk away, set boundaries, and prioritize our health. emotional, mental, and physical. Understanding that our need to be needed, liked, or desired is sometimes what keeps us stuck can be a life-changing realization. It doesn't mean we stop caring for others, but it does mean we stop letting their behavior dictate our peace. We have the power to say no. We have the right to walk away. We can choose ourselves.

The longer we remain in situations that drain us, the greater the risk to our well-being. But the moment we choose to let go is the moment we regain our power. Our peace, health, and happiness are more valuable than any unhealthy relationship or job. Once we realize this, we can begin the process of healing and moving forward, free from the burden of attachments to things that no longer serve us.

This chapter isn't about impulsively cutting people off. It's about understanding the dynamics of difficulty so you can guide yourself toward a calm, intentional, and fulfilling life. Let this be your wake-up call: You deserve peace. You deserve to feel safe in your mind. The first step? Know your cauliflower.

Chapter 4
The Permission to Not Align
Bias, Triggers, and the Courage to Leave with Integrity

We rarely discuss it openly, but every leader eventually faces the challenge of coaching or working with someone they just don't connect with. It might be a personality clash, their energy, tone, or the way they take up space in a room. Or it could be something subtle you can't quite identify, yet it still irritates.

And then comes self-doubt, the quiet, creeping kind that wraps around your thoughts and whispers things you've heard your whole life: "You're overreacting." "Be more patient." "Strong people rise above this." It tells you that disliking someone, even gently, even with respect, is a failure of character. A failure of leadership.

So, you bury it. You smooth your expression, force a smile, and do the work. You perform because that's what you've been taught to do. And under it all, you carry a silent weight, an ache you don't talk about. The burden of disliking someone you still have to work with, collaborate with, sit beside in meetings.

The burden of feeling something real and wondering if that makes you unkind.

That self-doubt is heavy. It convinces you that setting a boundary is selfish. That feeling of exhaustion by someone else's energy is a sign of weakness. That naming your discomfort makes you unprofessional. It twists emotional awareness into self-doubt, turning natural human reactions into hidden shame. You don't just question your judgment; you begin to question your right to feel what you feel. I know that burden well. It takes up space in the heart and mind until you finally realize: it's not your empathy that needs to change, it's the expectation that you must betray yourself to keep the peace.

For years, I worked in a role I absolutely loved. The work itself energized me. The team was sharp. The impact was real. On paper, it was a dream job.

But there was one problem: I didn't respect the leader of the organization. It wasn't a major issue or a single dramatic moment. It was a slow erosion of trust and respect. I didn't align with their values. I didn't admire their decision-making. I didn't feel inspired or seen. Over time, it became increasingly difficult to sit through meetings, contribute ideas, or even walk through the front door with the same enthusiasm I once had.

Each day, the job I loved started to feel heavier, not because the work had changed, but because I was carrying a secret. I don't like the person I'm supposed to be following. That secret weighed on me. I was afraid of being "found out." I feared that if I ever let the mask slip, if even a flicker of my true feelings showed, I'd be labeled insubordinate, difficult, or disloyal.

So I smiled. I nodded. I kept doing the work. But inside, I was quietly shrinking. I started to dread Mondays. My energy dipped. My creativity dried up. And the self-doubt only grew louder: "What kind of leader feels this way?" "You're supposed to rise above this." "Just try harder."

But the harder I tried to like this person, the more inauthentic I felt. And the more inauthentic I felt, the more disconnected I became, not just from them, but from myself.

That experience taught me something I have never read in a leadership manual: personal bias does not go away just because you deny it. You can convince yourself that you are fair, that you see the world clearly, that you are immune to the subtle influences that shape human behavior. But bias does not disappear in the face of denial. It simply sinks in deeper. It burrows into your thinking, into your instincts, into the very way you interpret the world around you. It makes a home beneath the surface, quietly influencing your reactions and choices without ever announcing itself.

Over time, this buried bias festers. It grows in darkness, fed by avoidance and ignorance. It begins to distort your perceptions. It whispers in your ear before you've even finished hearing someone's story. It shapes your expectations before you give someone a fair chance. It hardens your judgments. It builds walls between you and the people you might otherwise connect with. Festered bias starts to infect your relationships, your leadership, your friendships, and even your own self-image, often without you realizing how far it reaches.

If left unaddressed, bias doesn't stay inactive. It starts making decisions for you. It affects how you connect with others. It influences who you listen to and who you dismiss. It impacts how much effort you're willing to put into certain situations. It decides whether you open your heart completely or hold parts of yourself back out of distrust. It shapes the tone of your conversations, the energy you bring into a room, and the sincerity of your interactions. Without awareness, bias controls how much respect you show, how much forgiveness you give, and how much faith you have in those around you.

The danger isn't in having bias. Every person has bias because it's a natural result of life experiences, culture, upbringing, and personal wounds. The true risk is pretending bias doesn't exist within us. When we ignore it, we silently let it control our actions. It pulls the strings behind the scenes, making decisions for us while we think we're acting freely.

Addressing bias is not a source of shame or guilt. It is an act of true courage. It demands a willingness to look inward honestly and humbly. It asks us to examine the stories we've told ourselves about others and ourselves, and to consider whether those stories still serve us. It encourages us to replace judgment with curiosity, assumptions with questions, and defensiveness with openness. Confronting bias is the work of those who want to lead with integrity, love with sincerity, and build bridges instead of walls.

This work is challenging. It requires us to confront discomfort. It urges us to acknowledge that we may not be as neutral as we wish to believe. It calls us to take responsibility for recognizing that unconscious bias can cause harm even when it is not intentional. However, through this work, we gain freedom. We reclaim our ability to choose how to navigate the world, rather than being controlled by unseen fears and inherited stories. We create space for greater empathy, deeper connection, and communities built on trust instead of suspicion.

Every leader who aims to grow, evolve, and lead with integrity must ultimately face a moment of reckoning. It often comes quietly after a difficult conversation, following a tense meeting, or during a pause between responsibilities. It's the moment when external noise fades, and you realize the real work isn't just out there ,it's within. Growth doesn't start by pointing fingers or listing what others need to change. It begins when you ask a harder question: *What patterns am I repeating? What assumptions am I holding? What truth am I avoiding about how I lead, respond, and show up?*

This isn't about assigning blame. It's not about fixing yourself or feeling guilty. It's about having the courage to see yourself clearly, not through perfectionism or performance, but through curiosity and compassion. It's about recognizing the parts of you that still seek approval, the instincts that tighten in conflict, and the stories you tell yourself about what it means to lead well. It's about owning your impact, not just your intentions.

Leaders don't grow by chasing an ideal. They grow by being honest with themselves, especially when it's hard. They improve by noticing how they deflect, avoid, or justify and choosing instead to be truthful. Real leadership starts when you're willing to stop performing and begin listening, not just to others, but to yourself. Not to your loudest fears, but to the quiet voice of self-awareness that says: *This is where the work begins.*

At its core, leadership isn't just about managing others; it's about mastering yourself. True mastery depends on awareness. As mentioned previously, every leader has blind spots: parts of ourselves we don't easily see. These are habits, assumptions, reactions, and patterns that operate quietly beneath the surface. They affect how we speak, make decisions, respond under pressure, and connect with others. If left unchecked, blind spots can cause us to unintentionally harm, miss opportunities, and limit the potential of those we are meant to serve.

Blind spots often come to light through triggers. A trigger is a strong emotional response that seems out of proportion to the situation. It can be the flash of anger during a meeting when someone questions your idea. It might be the sudden defensiveness when a team member provides feedback. Or it could be the silent withdrawal when a colleague's style clashes with yours. Triggers are not random; they serve as clues.

They point to unresolved issues within us, signaling unmet needs, unresolved experiences, or beliefs about ourselves that make us feel threatened.

Facing your triggers requires humility. It asks you to pause before reacting and to ask deeper questions. What story am I telling myself about this situation? Where have I felt this feeling before? Is this reaction truly about what is happening now, or is it rooted in something older and deeper? Leaders who learn to get curious about their triggers rather than be controlled by them create a profound shift. They move from being reactive to being responsive. They build emotional resilience. They develop the self-awareness needed to navigate conflict with grace rather than fear.

Beyond blind spots and triggers lie what I call growth edges. Growth edges are the places where your next level of leadership is waiting. These are the spots where you stretch yourself beyond what's known, beyond what's comfortable, and often beyond what feels immediately possible. They aren't just about improvement or refinement; they're about expansion. These moments and spaces challenge your current skill set, mindset, or emotional bandwidth. Something more is being asked of you: more patience, more clarity, more presence, more courage. And while that invitation may come disguised as discomfort, tension, or resistance, it also serves as the gateway to your next evolution as a leader and as a person.

Stretching yourself at a growth edge doesn't mean forcing or pushing beyond your limits recklessly. It means choosing to lean into discomfort intentionally. It's the internal stretch, the kind that asks you to hold a difficult conversation you might have avoided before, to sit in ambiguity without rushing to fix, or to give someone else space to grow without stepping in to control the outcome. Stretching yourself might mean showing up vulnerable when it feels safer to stay guarded. It could mean loosening your grip on perfectionism to allow for more genuine connection. It might also mean risking being misunderstood to speak a deeper truth.

What makes growth edges hard is that they challenge your current identity. They question your internal story of who you are and how you lead. You might have always seen yourself as calm under pressure, but now you're being asked to be emotionally honest, not just composed. You may take pride in solving problems, but now you need to become a listener, a space-holder, a co-creator. These changes are tough and may not feel-good right away. However, they are vital if you want to grow into a version of yourself that is not just reactive but purposefully rooted in wisdom rather than habits.

Stretching yourself at a growth edge also requires discernment. It's not about taking on more than you should or proving your worth through over-functioning. It's about pausing long enough to ask: Where am I being asked to grow right now? What would it look like to meet this moment with more awareness, more curiosity, more strength? That kind of stretch is deeply personal and deeply transformational. It's not about becoming someone new; it's about becoming more fully yourself.

Ultimately, growth edges are where transformation occurs. Not all at once, but gradually, through deliberate choices and courageous moments. These edges are where your leadership transcends a title or a list of tasks. It becomes a reflection of who you are, stretched, evolving, and grounded in truth.

Self-reflection isn't a milestone you reach and then move past; it's a lifelong discipline. It's the ongoing, sometimes uncomfortable practice of looking inward with honesty and curiosity. It's the choice to ask yourself hard questions when it would be easier to assign blame, and to examine your own behavior when pointing outward feels more convenient. True leadership doesn't start with controlling others; it begins with understanding yourself. This kind of inner work isn’t a one-time event; it’s a daily posture. It’s the quiet decision to stay present to your own motivations, triggers, assumptions, and fears.

And here’s something essential to recognize: the moment you feel resistance, the urge to take the easier route, avoid the conversation, or postpone the decision, that's the moment to pay close attention. Resistance is often not a red flag but a compass. What we avoid most urgently is often where our greatest growth resides. When something challenges you, stirs discomfort, or brings up defensiveness, it’s usually because it’s touching a place that needs your attention. Not because you’re weak, but because you’re being asked to stretch. Choosing the easier path may feel safe in the moment, but it rarely leads to transformation. It keeps you protected, not empowered. That discomfort you’re tempted to run from? It may be the doorway to the exact breakthrough your leadership and your life are asking for.

Leaders who avoid this internal growth often become stiff over time. They start leading from ego instead of presence, more concerned with being seen as strong than being grounded in self-awareness. They unintentionally create environments where fear replaces trust, where people perform rather than participate, and where growth stalls because authenticity feels unsafe. Without regular inner reflection, unconscious patterns go unchecked and ultimately shape the culture around them.

But leaders willing to do this inner work, sit with discomfort, acknowledge bias, and take responsibility for how they move through the world. They build something entirely different. They create cultures of clarity, courage, and connection. They model what it looks like to learn, to grow visibly, and to lead from a place of deep integrity. Their power doesn't come from perfection. It comes from their ability to be real, to say this is where I'm learning, and to invite others to do the same.

This work isn't about shame or self-judgment. It's about reclaiming parts of yourself that have been running on autopilot. It's about breaking cycles you didn't even realize you were repeating. It's about having the courage to stay present with difficult things instead of bypassing or burying them. And it's about honoring the truth that personal bias doesn't disappear with good intentions; it dissolves through intentional, ongoing practice. Only by recognizing your blind spots, assumptions, and discomfort can you start to dismantle what no longer benefits you or those you lead.

Leadership rooted in self-awareness isn't static or formulaic. It's adaptable. It requires a daily embrace of truth, a willingness to see yourself clearly, to choose the more difficult path when growth calls for it, and to lead with a presence that refuses to sacrifice honesty for approval. When you live and lead from that place, you stop reacting and start responding. You stop performing and start transforming. You build trust not because you have all the answers, but because you're courageous enough to ask the right questions, especially of yourself.

This is the work. It's uncomfortable, humbling, and the start of everything that matters.

What finally helped me move forward was not forcing myself to like that leader. It was giving myself permission not to. It was admitting, privately at first, that I did not admire them. That I did not trust their leadership. That I could still respect their position without pretending to feel something I did not. That shift restored my integrity. Because integrity is not about pretending. It is about being honest with yourself and still choosing to act with fairness, consistency, and professionalism. It is about saying: I may not click with this person, but I can still do my job well. I can still show up with purpose. I can still treat them with respect.

For a long time, I resisted that truth within myself. I told myself that walking away would mean I could not persevere, that I was not strong enough to lead through discomfort. I worried about how it would look, especially as a leader, to admit that I did not want to be there anymore. We are taught to stay, to push through, to make it work. Particularly in leadership roles, we bear the extra burden of performance, driven by an internalized belief that if we walk away, we are letting others down or showing weakness. But here is the truth: sometimes leaving is the most honest, most self-respecting choice you can make. When you have tried, when you have shown up with fairness, when you have checked your biases and still experience that fundamental dissonance, and when the environment begins to undermine your sense of self, drain your energy, and steal your joy, staying can become a form of betrayal.

There is a moment, sometimes, amid all the wrestling with bias, expectations, and self-doubt, when a deeper truth begins to whisper through the noise. This environment no longer aligns with who I am becoming. That is not failure. That is clarity.

When I stopped trying to force personal alignment, I was able to regain my energy. I found peace in recognizing that you do not have to like someone to work with them. You do not have to fake connection to stay true to your role. And when it became clear that the disconnection was beginning to affect my sense of self, I decided to move on, not out of bitterness, but because it was the right choice. I left with clarity, not resentment.

The experience of leaving is rarely straightforward. It is layered, textured, and deeply human. On the surface, it may seem like a decision that is calculated, timely, even strategic. But underneath, it is a slow unraveling of who you have been and who you thought you should be. It is a quiet earthquake, invisible to most but felt throughout your entire being.

Even when you know it is time to go, even when your heart has been whispering for months that you have outgrown the space you are in, there is grief. A profound kind of grief that does not always show up as sadness. Sometimes it feels like exhaustion. Sometimes it hides behind relief. But it is there, in the spaces between your breaths, in the questions you ask yourself late at night. Did I give enough. Will I still matter when I am no longer in that role. Who am I without it.

Leaving is more than walking away from a job, a relationship, a role, or a routine. It is about shedding an identity that has been wrapped around you like a second skin. You remember how hard you worked to build it, how much time you spent convincing others and yourself that you were good at it, that you belonged. That version of you knew how to survive, how to deliver, how to rise. And now you are asking it to let go. That is not just a transition. That is a transformation.

There is doubt, too. Not because you've made the wrong choice, but because you are stepping into the space where the old no longer fits, yet the new hasn't fully arrived. It's disorienting. You wake up some mornings feeling the absence of structure. You miss the adrenaline rush of solving problems and the affirmation of being needed. You begin to see how much of your self-worth was tied to your performance, productivity, and usefulness to others. You grieve that. You mourn the parts of you that only came alive in response to pressure. And even though you know more awaits on the other side, the silence is deafening.

And then, slowly, something begins to shift. After the tears, after the numbing, after the anger and nostalgia and all the mixed-up feelings have had their say, you start to hear a quieter voice inside. One that was always there but got drowned out by the noise of proving and performing. This voice is gentler. Wiser. It doesn't ask for your credentials. It doesn't care about your calendar. It asks you what you love. What you long for. What you miss about yourself.

Releasing an identity is not a betrayal of who you were. It's an act of honoring the fact that you are allowed to evolve. What once served you may now be holding you back. A title or role, no matter how prestigious, is not your true self. Leaving something behind does not mean failure; it often means you've outgrown that chapter.

There is a sacredness in this kind of departure. A quiet courage in saying, "I am more than this." Not from arrogance, but out of reverence for your growth. It takes strength to walk away from something that offers structure but not wholeness. It takes grace to loosen your grip on the version of yourself that others relied on. And it requires deep, trembling faith to believe that what lies ahead is not emptiness, but expansion.

So, when you leave, honor what you've built. Mourn what you're letting go of. Bless the version of you who carried so much, who stayed so long, and who tried so hard. Then, with as much softness as you can muster, turn toward the unknown. That's where the truest version of you is waiting, not behind the mask of expectation, but in the raw, wild space of possibility.

What I've learned is this: there is nothing weak about honoring your limits. There is nothing shameful about recognizing when a system, a culture, or a relationship no longer allows you to thrive. Sometimes love for the work isn't enough to outweigh the energy it takes to endure an environment where you feel unseen or out of alignment. When you choose to leave, consciously, respectfully, and with integrity, honor yourself. You are not running away. You're returning to yourself. You're choosing truth over performance. Peace over politeness. Health over habit. That's not failure. That's leadership of the most personal kind.

Sometimes, the bravest thing you can do is walk away from something that looks right on paper but feels wrong in your soul. That's not giving up. That's knowing what you're worth. So, if you ever find yourself in that place, torn between staying in a space not meant for you any longer or stepping into the unknown, let this be your reminder: honoring yourself is always the right move. And it doesn't make you any less of a leader. If anything, it makes you more of one.

This book is about that moment of release. It's about the aching beauty of choosing yourself, even when the world has taught you otherwise. It's about closing a door with trembling hands and a fierce heart, trusting that whatever is waiting for you on the other side is not just new, but truly yours.

Chapter 5
Respect the Role Even If You Resist the Person

Let's be honest, genuinely and vulnerably honest. In an ideal world, every colleague would feel like an old friend. There would be effortless synergy, conversations that feel natural and energizing, and a shared rhythm that makes collaboration not just productive but joyful. We imagine teams where every meeting sparks ideas, every voice is in tune, and we leave the room feeling seen, understood, and valued. That's the dream.

But the real world isn't that simple, it is far more complex. It's made up of human beings who bring their own histories, temperaments, traumas, communication styles, and coping mechanisms into the room. And in that complexity, you'll inevitably find yourself working with someone who feels…off. Misaligned. Maybe they talk too much. Maybe they hardly talk at all. Maybe they drain the energy from the room just by entering, or maybe it's something more subtle: a tone, a posture, an energy that clashes with your own.

You might try to shake it off, give it time, or chalk it up to differences in style. Yet, despite your best efforts, the ease, the unspoken connection that makes teamwork feel natural, never quite comes. Instead, there's tension, distance, and a quiet but persistent sense of dissonance. With it often comes self-doubt. The inner dialogue begins: *Shouldn't I be able to get along with everyone? Am I being judgmental? Maybe I'm the problem.*

But here's the truth most leaders and professionals are afraid to admit: it's okay not to click with everyone. It's not a failure of character. It's not a sign of poor leadership. It's simply human. Chemistry isn't a guarantee; it's a bonus. And while it can make collaboration easier, its absence doesn't mean professional relationships are doomed to fail.

What matters more, infinitely more, is professional respect. The willingness to treat someone with dignity even when you don't understand them. The ability to recognize another person's strengths and contributions, even when their presence irritates or confuses you. The discipline to listen with patience, communicate clearly, and honor boundaries consistently, even when warmth feels unreachable.

There is something noble, something deeply mature about showing up fully for someone you don't naturally connect with. It requires restraint. It demands inner awareness. It involves the quiet inner work of asking, *"How can I rise above my preferences and act in alignment with my values?"* Because true leadership isn't based on chemistry. It's based on character.

And so, even when there's no spark, even when conversations feel forced and collaboration feels awkward, you can still lead with respect. You can still model grace. You can still hold space for someone's humanity, even when you don't feel attracted to their personality. That is the true test of leadership maturity.. Not how well you work with those you like, but how well you work with those you don't.

It doesn't mean forcing a friendship. It doesn't mean pretending. It means choosing professionalism over personal preference. It involves knowing when to set boundaries and when to soften them. And it means always remembering that shared respect can be just as strong a foundation as shared chemistry, possibly even more so. Because respect doesn't require liking someone; it requires valuing them. And that's a choice we can make, even when there's no connection. Especially then.

Respecting someone even when you do not like them is one of the clearest signs of emotional maturity. It means you recognize their skills, contributions, and worth as a professional without needing to feel personally connected. You don't have to force a friendship. You don't have to fake warm feelings. What you do need to do is treat them with dignity, fairness, and professionalism. Separating personal feelings from professional behavior is a skill that not only protects your integrity but also elevates the entire team's functioning. This is where inner awareness and resilience really come into play.

Treating someone with dignity means recognizing their inherent worth regardless of their role, performance, or personal challenges. It shows in small actions: listening without interrupting, acknowledging contributions in meetings, offering honest feedback without demeaning, and respecting personal boundaries even under pressure.

Practicing fairness involves applying standards consistently, making decisions based on merit rather than favoritism or politics. It includes setting clear expectations for everyone, providing opportunities fairly, and being transparent about how and why decisions are made. Fairness doesn't mean treating everyone exactly the same; it means treating everyone with equal consideration and honesty, while adapting to their individual needs and circumstances.

Professionalism is the unspoken agreement you have with yourself and those around you: to act with integrity, stay composed even during conflicts, focus on solutions instead of blame, and hold yourself responsible before blaming others. It also involves giving criticism kindly, standing up for yourself without being aggressive, and promoting your work without stepping on others.

When you practice dignity, fairness, and professionalism, you are not just doing a favor for others, you're strengthening your own leadership foundation. You maintain your self-respect. You foster emotional resilience. You create a leadership reputation based on trust instead of fear.

In a world where many leaders fall into patterns of reaction, ego, and pursuit of short-term wins, you become the steady force. Long after titles fade and achievements blur, people remember how it felt to work with you. When you treat others with dignity, you protect your own dignity. When you act fairly, you sleep well at night. When you embody professionalism, you attract a professional energy in return.

An organization is more than just a business entity; it's a living, breathing ecosystem composed of human beings. It is influenced not only by strategic plans or profit margins but also by the emotional and psychological experiences of the people who are part of it each day. Every hallway conversation, every performance review, and every team meeting contribute to an invisible web of human interaction. Like any ecosystem, the overall health depends on the integrity of its individual parts.

When dignity, fairness, and professionalism are placed at the core of a leadership culture, the effects extend far beyond policies or procedures. These principles become the soil in which trust takes root. They send a message spoken and unspoken that every person matters, not just for what they produce, but for who they are. Dignity reminds us to see the humanity in others, even when we disagree. Fairness ensures that decisions are grounded in consistency, not favoritism or bias. And professionalism sets the standard for how we navigate complexity, conflict, and communication with respect and maturity.

Leaders who prioritize these values do more than create a productive environment; they foster one that feels safe. A space where people feel valued, heard, and able to bring their full selves without fear of humiliation or harm. Psychological safety becomes the norm, not the exception. In that environment, innovation thrives. Collaboration deepens, and people start to take risks, not because they're reckless, but because they trust they won't be punished for being bold or vulnerable.

The cascade effect is real. When employees see fairness from leadership, they are more likely to act fairly toward one another. When they are treated with dignity, they start to show dignity outwardly, even in tough situations. Professionalism spreads not as a strict rule, but as a shared understanding of how people will treat each other during stress, urgency, and change.

And perhaps most importantly, when leadership models dignity, fairness, and professionalism, it helps shape the organization's identity itself. The culture becomes more than a poster on the wall or a slide in onboarding; it becomes a living ethos, evident in how people speak, listen, hold each other accountable, and repair when things go wrong.

In the absence of these values, organizations may survive but they will not thrive. Productivity may continue, but at a cost: morale erodes, retention suffers, innovation stalls, and mistrust spreads quietly through the ranks. But when dignity, fairness, and professionalism are deeply rooted, the organization becomes something more resilient, more sustainable, and far more human. It becomes a place where people don't just work, they belong. Treating people with dignity, fairness, and professionalism is similar to understanding how people feel about cauliflower. It might sound like a stretch at first, but the comparison offers more insight than it appears. Cauliflower is one of those foods people often have strong, personal reactions to. Some see it as a blank canvas, something that can be transformed into almost anything with the right preparation. Others find it plain, uninteresting, or even unpleasant, regardless of how it's served. And those opinions aren't random; they're shaped by memories, experiences, culture, and emotion.

For some, cauliflower evokes warm memories of family dinners and comforting meals. For others, it might be linked to less pleasant moments, like being forced to eat something they disliked or associating it with diets and restrictions. The key point is that no two people view it the same way. The same principle holds true in the workplace.

People bring their full selves to work, stories, preferences, fears, and hopes. If we expect everyone to show up, react, or participate identically, we overlook what makes them human. Just as insisting everyone enjoy cauliflower in the same way doesn't make sense, expecting uniformity in how people work or respond to leadership can be shortsighted.

Dignity involves recognizing that people may perceive the same environment very differently. Fairness in leadership is not about treating everyone the same, but about providing the support and expectations each person needs to succeed. And professionalism means respecting those differences, not judging them. It includes showing up consistently, communicating clearly, and making space for a variety of experiences.

When we lead with these values, we aren't just managing tasks; we're creating an environment where people can do their best work, even if their paths or preferences differ from ours. And when we recognize that not everyone experiences "cauliflower" the same way, we become more thoughtful, more effective, and more human in our leadership.

Connection by Choice

Cultivating Rapport When It Doesn't Come Naturally

Building rapport without personal chemistry isn't about putting on a mask or faking connection. It's not about forcing friendliness or pretending to feel something you don't. Instead, it's about practicing leadership maturity, learning how to manage your internal reactions while still showing empathy and professionalism. Leadership maturity encourages you to pause before reacting, to be curious instead of defensive, and to realize that someone else's behavior doesn't have to control your responses. It's the ability to separate temporary discomfort from your larger purpose.

At the core of this work is resilience, the quiet strength that lets you stay grounded and effective even when the environment feels tough. Resilience in leadership isn't about pushing through or suppressing your feelings; it's about managing them. It's the ability to handle uncomfortable interactions without taking them personally, to bounce back from tense moments without losing your balance. Resilient leaders don't let difficult dynamics control their tone or pull them off course. Instead, they stay true to their values and focus on the bigger picture, choosing growth, connection, and clarity even when it's challenging.

When personal chemistry is absent, interactions can feel draining, awkward, or unproductive. It's easy to disengage, shut down, or dismiss the other person as simply "difficult." But that's when leadership maturity and resilience are most important. Together, they enable you to approach others with consistent respect, even when you're not naturally drawn to them. You can set boundaries without appearing cold, express your thoughts without escalating conflict, and maintain rapport based on mutual purpose rather than personal preference.

Ultimately, building rapport in these situations is a deliberate act. It's about shifting your focus from "Do I like this person?" to "How can I show up in a way that reflects the leader I aspire to be?" That shift is powerful. It frees you from feeling like you must force chemistry and allows you to foster connection built on trust, respect, and shared goals. And over time, that kind of rapport, earned rather than assumed, can become even stronger than the kind that appears effortlessly.

One key technique for building resilience is accepting the situation for what it is. Not every connection is meant to feel natural, and that doesn't mean you're failing. It's simply part of being human. Acceptance helps you let go of unrealistic expectations and stop wasting energy trying to force something that isn't there. Another technique is staying focused on what you can control: your attitude, your tone, and your willingness to stay respectful and solution oriented. Practicing mindfulness can help you stay centered during difficult interactions. Reframing the relationship by emphasizing shared goals instead of personal differences helps you stay professional. Setting healthy internal boundaries is also essential.

Know your limits and protect your emotional energy without withdrawing into coldness or hostility.

Building rapport without personal chemistry often resembles consistent, steady professionalism. You communicate clearly. You listen actively. You acknowledge contributions. You approach others with fairness, patience, and a focus on the bigger picture. It doesn't mean forcing fake conversations or pretending you enjoy every interaction. It also doesn’t mean oversharing or trying to bond over things that feel unnatural. Authenticity still matters. You can be professional and kind without being fake or emotionally overextended.

But what do you do when it feels like everyone's cauliflower? When you look around and realize that every relationship feels strained, awkward, or draining? First, you pause. You remind yourself that patterns in relationships often reflect something deeper, either within the environment or within ourselves. If everyone feels difficult, it may be a sign that the culture around you is stressed, competitive, or dysfunctional. Or it might be a sign that your own emotional reserves are depleted, making even normal interactions feel heavier than they should.

In those moments, it's crucial to reinforce your resilience strategies. Prioritize self-regulation first.

Ensure you're getting enough rest, clarity, and emotional support outside of work. Don't take every challenging situation personally. Stay focused on your mission: What are you here to achieve? What do you want your energy to communicate about you, even when others are struggling to manage theirs? If the environment truly feels unhealthy beyond repair, it may be time to reconsider whether that space deserves your talents long-term. Sometimes, the best way to respect yourself is to recognize when a setting is no longer healthy for your growth. Showing up as your best self, regardless of who is beside you, involves holding to your standards of professionalism, kindness, and emotional steadiness, even if others behave differently. It includes listening carefully when someone speaks, even if you disagree, such as nodding and making eye contact when a colleague you dislike shares their ideas. It means communicating clearly and respectfully, even if frustration simmers beneath the surface, for example, sending a professional, focused email to clarify a project deadline instead of letting irritation show in your tone. It involves giving credit where it's due, publicly recognizing a difficult team member's contribution to a successful project rather than withholding praise due to personal feelings. It also entails offering assistance when needed, like sharing helpful resources with a coworker who has been struggling, even if you don't normally socialize with them. Showing up as your best self means keeping your tone balanced and your words deliberate, especially when challenged, such as calmly addressing a disagreement instead of resorting to sarcasm or passive aggression. It includes staying composed when others react emotionally, choosing curiosity over judgment, for example, asking clarifying questions rather than assuming bad intentions when someone's tone is sharp. It involves setting healthy boundaries without hostility, like respectfully declining last minute work requests that infringe on your limits rather than snapping or shutting down. It's about entering meetings with a mindset of collaboration rather than competition, willing to partner with someone you don't particularly like if it benefits the work. Remember, your integrity is yours to uphold; others' behavior can't take it away. Your best self isn't performative; it's a daily decision to anchor yourself in values like respect, patience, empathy, and personal accountability, even when no one else models them. True leadership, regardless of title, begins with mastering this.

Why does rapport matter so much? Because workplaces depend on relationships. Good rapport doesn't always mean deep personal friendships, but it does establish a foundation of trust, predictability, and cooperation. When people feel respected, they work harder, collaborate more effectively, and bring greater creativity and courage. Without rapport, even the most talented teams struggle. Misunderstandings increase. Conflicts linger. Trust diminishes. All of this slows work down and harms the culture. Conversely, when people treat each other with professionalism and basic respect, even without strong personal chemistry, the team remains healthy, focused, and resilient.

Ultimately, professional respect isn't about liking everyone. It's about showing up as your best self, regardless of who is beside you. It's about choosing professionalism over pettiness, patience over frustration, and maturity over emotional reactions. By doing so, you not only protect your own peace but also help foster an environment where excellent work and great people can thrive.

A Seat That Counts

Why Fairness Must Come Standard

Everyone deserves a fair seat at the table, not because they have proven themselves, earned your approval, or fit a particular mold, but because dignity is a basic human right. It should not be handed out selectively based on performance, likability, or loyalty. Instead, we offer it simply because we recognize our shared humanity. When dignity is present, people feel seen, valued, and safe enough to contribute. When it's absent, the entire foundation of leadership begins to crack.

Fairness does not require agreement. It doesn't mean you automatically trust someone or feel connected to them. Fairness isn't about treating everyone the same; it's about giving everyone an equal starting point. It's a conscious choice to begin with respect, even before someone has "proven" themselves. That means being open to who a person *is* before reacting to who you *think* they are. It means understanding that value can show up in quiet ways, unfamiliar formats, or stages. It also means letting go of the idea that worth must be earned, and instead choosing to see potential, even when it is still developing.

When you promote fairness, you create room for possibility. You enable people to develop their strengths. You open space for voices that are often ignored. You shift the culture from judgment to discovery. And perhaps most importantly, you remove the hidden barriers that often prevent people from fully stepping into their roles. Fairness is not soft leadership; it is strong, structured, and intentional leadership. It is a discipline, not a convenience.

Without fairness, leadership risks favoritism. Decisions begin to seem political rather than principled. Trust diminishes. Morale drops. Talent remains undiscovered. Without dignity, leadership turns into domination, creating a power dynamic where fear replaces engagement and silence replaces collaboration. And without professionalism, leadership becomes personal, where emotions and biases override values and standards.

But when fairness is prioritized as the non-negotiable standard, accountability becomes clearer. Growth becomes easier to achieve. Success becomes more sustainable. People thrive when they are seen as worthy from the beginning. They show up differently when they know they are not entering a room where they have to fight for basic respect.

Leaders set the tone, and fairness signals: *you matter here.* Not after you prove yourself or fit in, but from the moment you walk through the door. This kind of leadership doesn't just impact individuals; it transforms organizations from the inside out.

What Happens When Someone's Behavior Breaks Trust

Let's be honest, truly honest. Not everyone who gets a seat at the table chooses to honor it. Not everyone realizes the weight of that invitation. While many come with good intentions, a desire to grow, and respect for the collective space, some do not. Some abuse the opportunity. Some misuse their influence. Some erode the foundation of trust through patterns of dishonesty, cruelty, disengagement, or selfish behavior. They hurt others with their words, their actions, or their refusal to accept responsibility for the impact they cause.

This is the part of leadership that no one glorifies. The part that demands courage, clarity, and compassion equally. Because true leadership isn't just about inclusion, it's about protection. It's about creating space for growth, yes, but also safeguarding that space from being eroded. Fairness does not mean permission for harm. Dignity isn't a blank check for disrespect. Compassion isn't the same as passivity.

When someone repeatedly undermines the values of the team by belittling others, avoiding accountability, stirring conflict, or draining the collective energy, leaders must respond. Not react but respond.

Thoughtfully. Firmly. Humanely. Leadership doesn't mean allowing behavior that tears at the fabric of trust or safety. It involves knowing when to draw the line, and doing so not out of punishment, but from a deep and sacred commitment to protect the integrity of the space you are called to steward.

This is the heartbreak of leadership: knowing that you can believe in someone's potential and still part company. You can wish it had gone differently and still make the decision to protect the team. You can extend chances, support, feedback, and coaching, then recognize when it's not being received. Leadership requires you to walk a fine line between empathy and enabling. Between understanding someone's story and refusing to let that story become an excuse for harm.

When someone's behavior clearly shows they are unwilling or perhaps unable to engage with respect, accountability, and care, the most loving and responsible action for leadership is to intervene. Not impulsively. Not vindictively. But with clarity. Using documentation, transparency, and determination. Because protecting the team is not the opposite of fairness; it is fairness in action.

And here's what's powerful: when leaders hold the line, they are not just managing a person; they are setting a tone. They are telling everyone at the table, *you matter. Your safety matters. Your energy, effort, and emotional well-being all matter here.* That is what builds true trust, not a fantasy of harmony, but a commitment to justice. Not tolerance for everything, but alignment with what the team stands for.

Because trust isn't built through endless accommodation. It develops when people see that the standards are real, that they are enforced, and that they serve the collective good. That's what transforms a group of individuals into a community. That's what makes a seat at the table not just symbolic but sacred.

The Balance of Leadership

Compassion with Boundaries

At the core of strong leadership is the ability to balance accountability and compassion to create an environment where fairness, professionalism, and dignity not only exist but work together. This is where the true work of leadership resides. Not in striving for perfection or popularity, but in navigating complexity with integrity.

Fairness involves creating conditions where someone truly has a chance to succeed. That includes setting clear expectations, providing timely and constructive feedback, offering meaningful support, and giving the opportunity to grow and adjust. It's not just about giving someone a seat; it's about giving them the tools and clarity to use that seat effectively.

Professionalism requires more. It demands that you respond when someone's behavior starts to compromise the integrity of the team or the safety of the environment. That response might involve coaching, redirection, a change in responsibilities, or if needed, separation from the role. Leadership is not passive. It does not wait and hope that issues resolve themselves. Instead, it entails taking deliberate action to safeguard the trust and well-being of the group.

And even then, dignity does not vanish. It stays a guiding principle, even in tough moments. You address the behavior, not attack the person. You remain focused on what the team needs, not in resentment or revenge. When a decision is made to change someone's role or end their participation, it can be done without humiliation or blame. Dignity isn't about avoiding discomfort, it's about choosing humanity, even when firmness is necessary.

The truth is, a seat at the table is a beginning, not a guarantee. It symbolizes belief in someone's potential and the offer of inclusion. But what a person does with that seat, how they show up, how they engage, and how they contribute determines whether they stay part of that space. Leadership honors that process by being fair, clear, and willing to act when the collective health of the team is at risk.

Protecting the integrity of the table isn't about excluding anyone; it's a pledge to everyone who earns their spot through effort, responsibility, and care. Holding the line isn't about turning people away. It's about maintaining a safe environment for those who are present. That is true leadership: balancing grace and strength, keeping doors open while setting clear boundaries, believing in people and respecting limits.

Leadership requires holding both truths at once:

Everyone is worthy of dignity.

Dignity does not mean tolerating harm.

Fairness means treating everyone equally. Professionalism involves applying those standards consistently. Dignity is remembering that even if someone loses their position, they still deserve respect. This is where leadership goes beyond authority and leaves a lasting impact.

At its core, leadership isn't just about achieving results; it's about *how* you achieve them. Every interaction, every decision, every conflict navigated serves as a small testament to your values. And among the most powerful yet often overlooked values are dignity, fairness, and professionalism.

Chapter 6
Conflict Isn't the Enemy
Reframing Conflict as a Path to Stronger Coaching Moments

We often see conflict as a sign that something is broken, that something has gone wrong, or that someone has failed, whether in communication, behavior, or leadership. But what if conflict isn't a red flag to avoid but a doorway to walk through? What if, when handled with intention and respect, conflict becomes one of the most powerful coaching tools available to leaders? In reality, conflict isn't the enemy; avoidance is.

Conflict in healthy relationships, whether professional or personal, is unavoidable and necessary. Consider this: conflict only occurs when people care. When values conflict, expectations differ, or communication fails, conflict appears to reflect underlying issues. It exposes frustrations, misalignments, and misunderstandings, providing an opportunity to address them directly. When combined with respect and emotional regulation, conflict becomes not just manageable, but also meaningful.

Some conflicts are loud and obvious, while others are quiet and hard to name. Whether conflict appears as disagreement, tension, resistance, or silence, it is always present in leadership. The most effective leaders are not those who avoid conflict, but those who can identify it, respond to it, and take responsibility for their role in it.

There are several types of conflict that leaders regularly face. Each one influences trust, participation, and culture in different ways. When left unresolved, they gradually weaken morale. When handled with self-awareness and skill, they become opportunities to strengthen leadership impact and relational integrity.

Role conflict occurs when a leader's responsibilities, expectations, or priorities are unclear or conflicting. A leader might be expected to be highly strategic while also handling daily operations or asked to advocate for their team while enforcing decisions they had no role in making. These tensions lead to burnout and confusion. To manage role conflict, leaders should ask clarifying questions, have honest conversations about priorities, and speak up when expectations become unrealistic. Taking responsibility means recognizing where confusion exists and seeking alignment instead of silently bearing the consequences.

Interpersonal conflict occurs between people who work closely together. It often emerges from clashing personalities, poor communication, or issues left unaddressed. Leaders may notice these tensions and hope they resolve on their own, but silence rarely brings relief. More often, it allows resentment to deepen and positions to harden.

Addressing interpersonal conflict requires leaders to engage directly and respectfully, while also examining their own role in the dynamic. Accountability might sound like acknowledging where clarity was missing or where feedback landed differently than intended, followed by a willingness to reset and move forward together.

Values conflict happens when someone's personal or professional beliefs clash with the organization's direction or culture. These conflicts are often complicated and emotionally intense. Leaders need to listen carefully, clarify their intentions, and, if necessary, question whether a process or decision truly represents the organization's core values. This kind of conflict requires leaders to stay true to their integrity and be willing to have tough conversations, even when it challenges the status quo.

Resource conflict occurs when there isn't enough time, staff, budget, or support to meet expectations. Teams may start to feel competitive, isolated, or frustrated. A leader's role is to promote transparency in decision-making, clearly communicate what is achievable, and acknowledge the impact of scarcity. Accountability in this situation might involve admitting when resources were poorly managed or unevenly distributed and taking steps to correct it.

Identity conflict occurs when people feel unseen, misunderstood, or diminished because of who they are rather than what they do. It often surfaces when values clash, perspectives are dismissed, or lived experiences are minimized, leaving individuals questioning their worth or place. These moments ask leaders to slow down, listen without defensiveness, and reflect on how their own assumptions or blind spots may be shaping the interaction. Accountability in this context means being willing to learn, acknowledge harm when it occurs, and respond in ways that restore trust and mutual respect.

Internal conflict is the private tension within a leader. It may manifest as imposter syndrome, fear of failure, or unresolved self-doubt. These conflicts can quietly influence how leaders make decisions, manage others, and perform under pressure. Managing internal conflict involves cultivating self-awareness, seeking coaching or support, and knowing when to pause and reflect before reacting. Accountability in this context is personal. It means recognizing your own limits and maintaining your leadership presence, not just your performance.

Each of these conflict types demands something different from a leader. Sometimes the task is to step in. Other times, it is to step back and reflect. In every case, leadership starts with accountability. It begins by asking, "What is this conflict asking of me?" and by being open to hearing the answer.

The key is reframing. Instead of asking, "Why is this happening to me?" or "How do I make this go away?" a grounded leader asks, "What is this conflict trying to show me?" and "How can I use this moment to coach, guide, or deepen understanding?" Reframing conflict begins with recognizing that it does not have to mean fighting. It can mean facing tension, truth, or an opportunity to realign and reset. Coaching through conflict is not about dominating or silencing. It is about navigating with clarity, empathy, and accountability.

Before you can reframe a conflict, you must ground yourself. Emotional regulation is the foundation of reframing. You cannot bring perspective if you are flooded with defensiveness or anger. The nervous system must settle first. That may mean pausing before responding, taking a breath, or naming your emotion, such as "I feel dismissed" or "I feel caught off guard," and then letting that awareness guide your next move rather than control it.

Grounding also means remembering your role. You are here to lead, not to win. You are here to create conditions where growth can happen, even amid disagreement.

Poorly handled conflict leads to power struggles. Well-managed conflict causes power shifts, where power is shared through clarity, boundaries, and mutual understanding. In moments of conflict, a great coach doesn't take things personally. Instead, they become curious. They ask more questions than they make accusations. They explain the "why" behind their feedback. They distinguish facts from feelings and demonstrate what it looks like to remain calm, direct, and respectful under pressure. Every effectively managed conflict leaves the door open for learning, trust, and accountability. And, of course, it wouldn't be this book without a cauliflower moment.

Reframing conflict is similar to trying to roast cauliflower for someone who believes they hate it. You know there's something valuable and nourishing in it, but they only see it as a mushy and flavorless disappointment. Conflict works the same way. If you've only experienced conflict as yelling, shutdowns, or retaliation, you'll naturally want to avoid it. It won't seem worth the trouble. But when approached differently, when it's seasoned with respect, slowly roasted with care, and the heat is kept controlled, conflict, like cauliflower, can transform. It becomes something easier to digest, more useful, and maybe even surprisingly satisfying.

The point isn't to force people to like conflict. The point is to help them stop fearing it. When leaders show that conflict isn't an ending but a beginning, they transform the emotional culture of the workplace. They shift the expectation from avoiding conflict to approaching it with curiosity, from silence to skill-building. When leaders face conflict honestly, they foster a culture of trust and resilience. Conflict then becomes a teacher rather than a threat. It uncovers what matters, what needs fixing, and what must change. Beneath every organization's surface lies a web of unspoken tensions. The strongest leaders are those who are willing to identify these tensions and take responsibility for moving through them with courage. And here's the truth: the best coaching often happens in tense, not tidy, moments. When a mistake occurs. When opinions clash. When feedback stings. These are the moments when character is built, not because you avoided the hard conversation but because you face it with composure, clarity, and care.

Conflict isn't the enemy. It's the fire that shapes leadership into something genuine.

The Role of Defensiveness in Conflict

If conflict is a fire that can shape leadership, then defensiveness is the wind that spreads it into a wildfire. It is one of the most common obstacles to meaningful conflict resolution and often, it appears suddenly and unexpectedly. You can be fully committed to handling conflict professionally and still feel defensiveness rising before the conversation even truly begins.

Defensiveness is a way of protecting yourself. It's the nervous system's method of putting up a shield when it perceives a threat to your competence, character, belonging, or sense of control. It might show up as justification, shutting down, sarcasm, interrupting, or blaming others. Sometimes it's loud and reactive, other times it's quiet and simmering. Either way, it can accidentally send a clear message: *I'm not listening. I'm protecting myself.* The tricky part is that defensiveness often feels justified in the moment. It seems like you're standing up for yourself. But in fact, it often closes the door to real dialogue. It blocks insight. It turns coaching into combat. And worst of all, it often produces the opposite of what you want:

disconnection instead of understanding, escalation instead of resolution, and isolation instead of collaboration.

Understanding why defensiveness occurs is the first step in reducing it. For many high-performing professionals, being wrong doesn't just challenge their ego; it threatens their sense of identity. The fear of judgment can also add to this, especially when someone already feels insecure in their role or unheard in a conversation. In those moments, feedback may seem more like a personal attack than an opportunity to grow. Past experiences also shape reactions. If previous conflicts involved humiliation, punishment, or dismissal, the nervous system remembers this. Even a well-meaning discussion can feel like a trap. Power dynamics make things more complicated. When someone feels powerless, they might use defensiveness to regain control or dignity, even if it's not appropriate. Lastly, perfectionism is a common trigger. When self-worth is closely tied to performance, even small critiques can trigger a strong fight-or-flight response.

To navigate defensiveness in yourself or others, lead with curiosity rather than control. Ask: *What's underneath this response? What fear might be driving this?* A defensive reaction doesn't mean someone is uncoachable; it means they're feeling exposed. And exposure without safety rarely leads to growth. For yourself, practicing emotional regulation techniques like pausing before responding, naming what you're feeling, and breathing intentionally can help lower the internal alarm. Defensiveness loses power when it's recognized and owned. You can say: *"I notice I'm feeling defensive right now. I want to hear you clearly, so I need a moment."* That single moment of self-awareness can change the entire trajectory of a conversation.

The goal isn't to eliminate defensiveness since we're all human. The goal is to recognize when it's present and choose to lead from a position of strength, not reaction. Because when you remove defensiveness, even briefly, what remains is clarity. And from clarity, true coaching becomes possible.

Conflict at Home

When Good Intentions Aren't Enough

Conflict doesn't pause when we leave work; it follows us into our homes, our relationships, and the quiet spaces where we should feel safest. In our personal lives, it often feels more complex, more vulnerable, and more tender. That's because personal conflict touches the parts of us connected to love, loyalty, identity, and trust. It's easy to believe that conflict in close relationships means something is wrong. Many of us have been taught to equate peace with love and conflict with failure. But the truth is, conflict itself isn't inherently unhealthy. It can signal people trying to grow together, values clashing, or unmet needs finding their voice. Conflict can be a sign, not a sentence. How we handle it determines whether it leads to connection or disconnection.

When we face conflict with good intentions, we come to the table genuinely wanting to understand rather than win. We choose curiosity over criticism. We see the other person not as an enemy but as someone we care about, even when we're frustrated. This involves asking questions like, "Can you help me understand how you're feeling" instead of defaulting to accusations such as, "You always do this." It also requires staying grounded enough to respond with kindness, even when emotions are strong. Additionally, it's important to check in with ourselves first and ask whether we are emotionally ready to engage with compassion and clarity. Good intentions don't mean sugarcoating the truth or avoiding difficult conversations. They mean telling the truth while honoring the dignity of the relationship. They involve being open to being wrong, willing to listen, and committed to repairing the relationship rather than holding on to pride.

However, not all conflict is the same. Some conflicts come from misunderstandings and can be fixed with empathy and good communication. But sometimes, what we call conflict is actually a pattern of unhealthy behavior. These are not just isolated disagreements; they are ongoing patterns that erode your self-worth and well-being. Emotional abuse, manipulation, gaslighting, persistent disrespect, and emotional neglect are not normal forms of conflict. They are harmful. In situations like these, the goal shifts from repair to release. Letting go of a personal relationship is one of the hardest decisions to make. Whether it is romantic, familial, or platonic, walking away can feel like giving up. It can seem like personal failure or betrayal of loyalty. But choosing to walk away is sometimes the most honest and brave act of self-respect.

Honoring your feelings means trusting them. If you often feel unseen, diminished, blamed, or emotionally drained when you're around someone, that is not something to ignore. Your discomfort is not drama; it is data, information from your nervous system about what isn't working. You are allowed to make choices that prioritize your peace, confidence, and emotional safety. Emotional safety is not a luxury in relationships; it is non-negotiable. You deserve relationships where your voice is heard, boundaries are respected, and your wellness isn't sacrificed for someone else's comfort. You can care and still let go, grieve and still protect your peace, wish someone well and walk away. Sometimes, love means choosing to love yourself first.

Conflict isn't a detour from connection; it can serve as a bridge to deeper understanding when approached intentionally. In both our professional and personal lives, our way of engaging with conflict reflects our emotional maturity, self-awareness, and core values. Responding to tension with curiosity instead of control, managing defensiveness, and leaning into clarity rather than chaos opens the door to true growth. Not every relationship endures conflict, but those that do often emerge stronger. Conversely, when relationships must end, we can exit with dignity by choosing peace over persistence. The aim isn't to eliminate conflict entirely but to transform it into a tool for coaching, a mirror for reflection, and a protector of our emotional safety. Through this approach, we grow not just as leaders but as human beings.

Repair and Rebuild

The Work After the Words

Conflict is never just about what happens in the moment. It's also about what happens afterward, in the quiet space where emotions begin to settle, reflection takes hold, and relationships either fracture or start to heal. No matter how honest or well-intentioned a difficult conversation may be, it leaves an emotional mark. That mark needs attention. Repair is the bridge between conflict and connection. It's not about erasing what happened but about acknowledging it with care. It's a way of saying, "We went through something hard, and I am still here. I want to move forward with you."

In professional environments, repairing relationships often requires leaders to take the initial step. This might involve reaching out to a colleague after a tense meeting to say, "I want to make sure we're okay. I know that conversation was tough, and I'm open to hearing how it landed for you." It could also mean sending a follow-up in writing to clarify intentions, show appreciation for their honesty, or invite continued dialogue. Repairing doesn't mean taking responsibility for everything that went wrong; it's about acknowledging your impact and showing openness instead of defensiveness.

In personal relationships, repair often starts with presence. It could be a softer tone of voice, a quiet act of kindness, or a message that says, "Can we talk when you're ready?" Sometimes it's an honest statement like, "I've been thinking about what I said, and I realize how that may have hurt you. That wasn't my intention, but I take responsibility for it." Repair is not always grand or dramatic. It is built through small gestures, moments of humility, and emotional honesty.

Rebuilding, however, is different from repair. Repair is an apology. Rebuilding is the consistency that comes afterward. Rebuilding shows that you have heard the other person and are willing to change the pattern, not just fix the moment. It involves creating new norms, establishing healthier rhythms, and setting clearer boundaries. It means choosing to stay in the relationship with clarity and intention, rather than out of habit or avoidance.

In both professional and personal relationships, rebuilding takes time. It requires effort from both people. One person alone cannot carry the weight of repair. Rebuilding involves checking in again, staying aware of emotional shifts, and following through on promises. It means letting the other person feel safe again, not just because you said the right words, but because you've shown up differently over time. Sometimes, even with the best intentions and effort, the other person may not be ready to repair or rebuild. They might need more time, or they might not be willing. That is something to accept without resentment. Repair is about offering healing, not forcing a resolution. You can take responsibility for your part, extend the invitation, and still release the outcome with grace.

Whether at work or at home, leadership is most visible after conflict. It reveals itself in what we do next. Not just in the apology, but in the habits that follow. Not in how we clean up the conversation, but in the culture we build afterward. Healing doesn't happen during the height of conflict. It takes place in the quiet days and weeks that come after. It shows in how we return, how we listen, and how we change.

When The Bridge Doesn't Need Repairing

There comes a moment in leadership when you look across a fractured professional relationship and realize you're the only one still there with a toolbelt, trying to rebuild the bridge. You've shown up with empathy. You've stayed late, listened longer, softened your approach, reworded your feedback, checked your tone. You've wondered what you could have done differently. And still, on the other side: silence. Resistance. Or worse, passive compliance cloaked in a smile. It's in that moment that an uncomfortable truth begins to rise: you may be trying to repair something that no longer serves you.

For a long time, I believed that every strained relationship at work was a test of my leadership. To be a strong, capable, emotionally mature leader, I had to *keep trying.* I thought tenacity equaled growth. That forgiveness, strategy, and a calm tone would eventually lead to reconciliation. But I've learned the difference between repairing and resurrecting. One is grounded in mutual respect; the other is an exercise in futility. Not every professional relationship can or should be saved. And that doesn't mean you've failed. Sometimes, the most mature, grounded decision a leader can make is to stop pouring energy into a container with no bottom. You don't owe your peace to every professional relationship. You don't owe your energy to someone committed to misunderstanding you. And you certainly don't owe your leadership capital to someone who has already emotionally opted out of mutual trust and respect.

We have limited time, energy, and endless responsibility. Leadership isn't about making everyone like or agree with you. It's about leading with clarity, consistency, and care, even when it means knowing when a bridge isn't worth rebuilding. This is where your leadership compass becomes crucial. Your principles and *non-negotiables* will guide you here. If you've acted in line with those values and there's no mutual effort to repair, then you can let go of it. With grace, clarity, and peace.

Releasing does not mean retaliation.
It does not mean unprofessionalism or cruelty.
It means acceptance.

Acceptance that some people will cast you as the problem, no matter how generously you invite collaboration. Acceptance that your leadership will not resonate with everyone. And acceptance that not every damaged relationship needs restoration, especially when repair requires you to betray yourself.

What if, instead of pushing harder to win someone over, you redirected that energy toward the people and projects where trust is mutual and growth is possible? What if you allowed some professional dynamics to remain unresolved, not out of bitterness, but out of respect for your own energy?

This, too, is leadership.

Chapter 7
Bridging the Gap
Navigating Conflict in a Multi-Generational Workforce

Today's workforce is more generationally diverse than ever before. Traditionalists, Baby Boomers, Generation X, Millennials, and Generation Z often collaborate on the same project teams, share messages in common inboxes, and participate in the same meetings. Each generation brings its own life experiences, values, and ideas of success. Each has been influenced by different social, economic, and technological realities.

This convergence holds great promise. The extensive institutional knowledge of experienced employees, combined with the adaptability and fresh ideas of younger professionals, can foster innovation, creativity, and effective mentorship within organizations. When used wisely, generational diversity becomes a competitive advantage. It strengthens teams, broadens perspectives, and helps organizations stay grounded in experience while remaining adaptable to change.

Yet, alongside this opportunity, there is a complex challenge. These same generational differences can cause friction. Communication styles vary widely. While one generation may prefer face-to-face conversations, another might find texting or digital communication more effective. Work styles can differ in pace, process, and preferences for independence or teamwork. Feedback expectations may range from formal reviews to casual coaching. Even basic assumptions about professionalism, dress code, punctuality, and meeting manners, can lead to misunderstandings.

However, one of the most important commitments leaders must make is to avoid stereotyping people based solely on their birth year. Not every Gen Z employee desires digital only interaction. Not every Baby Boomer resists change. Assuming that people behave or think a certain way just because of their generational label oversimplifies the rich complexity of individual identity. It reduces human potential to a category and, in doing so, fosters unnecessary limitations and biases in the workplace.

Generational labels can provide insight, but they should never become a box that defines how someone is perceived or valued. We must prioritize seeing people first as individuals, with their own strengths, preferences, and motivations. While age or generational identity may influence a person's perspective, it should never be used to predict or judge it.

When organizations foster genuine dialogue and shared understanding, something powerful unfolds. Teams start to value not only what each person contributes but also why they do so. They learn to appreciate context as much as content. Mutual respect grows when employees are encouraged to share their preferences and are met with curiosity instead of assumptions.

To bridge generational gaps, leaders need to be deliberate. They should demonstrate open-mindedness, ask insightful questions, and avoid the comfort of stereotypes. Organizations need to invest in cross-generational learning opportunities, shared goal-setting, and inclusive communication practices.

This isn't about demanding conformity. It's about inviting connection. The most effective workplaces today recognize generational differences not as problems to fix but as a diverse array of perspectives to embrace. When we handle this complexity with care, humility, and a focus on dignity, we build cultures where everyone, regardless of age or background, feels seen, heard, and valued.

Beyond the Surface

Understanding the Quiet Impact of Generational Tension

Generational conflict in the workplace is rarely loud or dramatic. More often, it quietly simmers beneath the surface. It grows through small moments of misunderstanding, subtle tension, or silent frustration. It appears in eye rolls during meetings, in familiar refrains that resist change, or in assumptions about what people can or cannot handle. These interactions may seem minor on their own, but over time they gather and begin to influence the emotional climate of a team.

These conflicts often stem from differences in communication styles. One person might prefer direct conversations, while another feels more comfortable sharing thoughts through writing. Some may prioritize quick responses, whereas others need more time to think. Even tone, word choice, and punctuation can cause tension. What one person considers efficient, another might see as rushed. What one finds respectful, another could see as overly formal.

Misunderstandings occur when we expect others to follow our unspoken rules. A colleague might feel dismissed if an idea is ignored without discussion. Another could feel frustrated if their suggestions are questioned or reinterpreted. When these moments go unaddressed, they can create emotional distance. People begin to believe that others do not value their contributions or understand their way of working.

This tension can gradually erode a sense of belonging. When employees feel that their working style is consistently misunderstood or misrepresented, they may withdraw. When frustration is directed at how someone communicates or organizes their work, it implies that difference is a flaw rather than a strength. Over time, this fosters an environment where people participate less, speak less freely, and take fewer creative risks.

The impact isn't always immediately obvious, but it's real. Collaboration starts to feel draining instead of inspiring. Trust weakens. People begin to prioritize comfort over growth. Teams lose the advantage of their diverse perspectives because assumptions replace genuine dialogue.

Addressing this kind of conflict requires more than superficial fixes. It involves intention, empathy, and a shared dedication to listening without judgment. It means asking questions instead of making assumptions, clarifying expectations instead of defending habits, and remaining open to the idea that our way is not the only way.

When we begin to see differences as opportunities for understanding instead of sources of irritation, something changes. People feel acknowledged and understood. Teams operate more smoothly with greater mutual respect. The workplace becomes not just a space for productivity but a place of inclusion and connection.

To lead effectively across generations, the first step is awareness. Generational dynamics are real. They are not just personality differences or labels. They reflect life experiences, cultural shifts, and the pace of change that shape how people work, connect, and lead. These differences influence how individuals see the world, how they relate to authority, how they define purpose, and how they engage with others in the workplace.

For leaders, recognizing these differences is not enough. They must also understand how these dynamics influence culture, daily interactions, relationships, and overall team engagement. Leadership cannot be inflexible. What motivates one person might seem unimportant to another. What feels like recognition to one employee could seem impersonal to someone else.

These differences impact every aspect of the employee experience. They shape how people prefer to give and receive feedback, resolve conflicts, define accountability, and seek support. Some employees value structure and clear guidance, while others thrive with flexibility and autonomy. Some want frequent updates and real-time collaboration, whereas others prefer space to think, reflect, and then respond.

Communication is one of the most visible and misunderstood areas influenced by generational differences. It's not just about words but also about timing, tone, tools, and interpretation. What seems professional and respectful to one team member might feel cold or too formal to another. Some people prefer emails with concise bullet points, while others want a quick face-to-face check-in or a message through a collaborative platform. Some employees value direct, immediate feedback, while others need time to process before engaging in conversation.

These preferences are not about right or wrong. They focus on clarity, context, and culture. When communication is misaligned, assumptions form. People start to misinterpret intentions. They might disengage, second-guess, or feel left out. When communication breaks down, trust also diminishes.

Leaders must be intentional communicators. This involves understanding how each person best receives information. It includes clarifying expectations, listening for what isn't said, and adjusting the way you communicate to fit the audience's needs. Consistency is important, but so is flexibility. The aim is not to communicate more, but to communicate more effectively.

When leaders overlook generational dynamics, tension gradually builds. Meetings may seem unproductive. Collaboration can become strained. Employees might feel unseen or undervalued. Over time, these small frictions lead to a disconnect between people and purpose. The energy shifts. What once felt like a shared mission starts to feel like separate paths.

To lead effectively, leaders must shift from assumptions to curiosity. They need to be willing to step outside their comfort zones and listen to how others work and think. They should be students of people, not just enforcers of process. This type of leadership doesn't require pleasing everyone; it demands presence, empathy, and humility to adapt.

The goal is not to erase generational differences, but to understand and respect them. When leaders create cultures that foster collaboration, value different perspectives, and communicate thoughtfully, the workplace becomes more unified, adaptable, and innovative.

Generational diversity isn't a problem to fix; it's a resource to nurture. Leading through it isn't about discovering the perfect strategy, but about showing awareness, listening intentionally, and responding respectfully. Think of a head of cauliflower. At first glance, it looks uniform, but up close, each floret varies slightly in shape. Some are packed tightly, while others are more loosely arranged. Each grows from the same stem but takes its own unique form.

This is how a multigenerational workforce operates. Everyone is united by a shared purpose, but each person offers a different perspective, rhythm, and way of contributing. Strong leadership involves recognizing and respecting these differences, rather than trying to make everyone the same.

Communication is the foundation that holds everything together. When it is clear and adaptable, the team remains connected. When it breaks down, the structure weakens.

Leadership across generations isn't about control; it's about cultivation. Like cauliflower, a team prospers when each part is encouraged to grow in its own way, together, with purpose.

When Communication Breaks Down

Leading Through Resistance

One of the most harmful communication conflicts in the workplace happens when leaders refuse to recognize the realities of a multigenerational workforce. Whether driven by habit, bias, fear of change, or a belief that leadership should stay the same regardless of the situation, this resistance causes a gap between leaders and the people they are supposed to support.

When leaders ignore generational differences, they often resort to one-way communication styles. They depend on outdated channels, tone-deaf messaging, or rigid expectations that no longer connect with large parts of the workforce. Instead of embracing curiosity, they default to criticism. Instead of adapting, they demand conformity. Over time, this results in silence, avoidance, and disengagement across teams.

What This Conflict Looks Like

- Team members feel hesitant to speak up because their ideas are regularly dismissed or misunderstood
- Employees receive unclear or inconsistent feedback that does not match their working style

- Leaders often mistake requests for flexibility or clarity as entitlement or insubordination
- Communication flows downward only, with little opportunity for shared dialogue
- Innovation slows because team members stop contributing new perspectives
- Trust erodes as employees feel unseen or undervalued

This kind of resistance does not just frustrate individual employees; it causes a ripple effect throughout the entire organization. When people perceive communication as one-sided, they stop investing emotionally. They hesitate to take creative risks and begin withholding feedback. Collaboration becomes cautious, and psychological safety declines.

The result is a culture that appears compliant on the surface but is quietly falling apart internally. Employees may stay, but they are no longer fully engaged. Teams may meet, but ideas remain small. Over time, the organization loses its ability to adapt because it cannot listen to itself think.

Curiosity is a leader's most effective tool here. Asking team members how they prefer to communicate, solve problems, or receive feedback helps reveal generational needs respectfully. Leaders might say, "Tell me how you like to work best. What helps you feel productive and supported?" These conversations promote understanding rather than judgment.

Leaders also need to establish clear communication norms. Without shared expectations, people will rely on their generational habits. Defining what belongs in an email versus a chat message, how often meetings are held, or how feedback is given helps reduce assumptions. When people understand what to expect, they feel more secure to contribute.

Reverse mentoring is a powerful approach. It enables younger employees to teach more experienced team members about new technology or trends, while also gaining insights from their institutional knowledge and experience. This exchange reduces generational hierarchies and fosters mutual respect. It reminds everyone that wisdom and innovation are not limited by age; they are shared responsibilities.

Generational bias is one of the most subtle and often overlooked forces that influence how leaders see, judge, and interact with their teams. It resides in casual comments like, *"She's too young to lead that project,"* or *"He's been here forever, but he's set in his ways."* It appears in performance reviews that unconsciously favor familiarity over innovation, or in hiring choices that prioritize "culture fit" instead of culture growth.

Leaders often hold internalized narratives about each generation. Millennials are seen as overly idealistic, Gen Z is considered lacking resilience, Gen X is viewed as cynical, and Boomers are perceived as resisting change. These stereotypes are rarely challenged because they have been normalized through media, repetition, and personal experience. However, when leaders fail to question these assumptions, they overlook the true talent, values, and potential standing right in front of them.

What Generational Bias Looks Like in Leadership

Generational bias in leadership often manifests in subtle yet powerful ways that affect how individuals are treated, valued, and developed within an organization. A common example is assumptive delegation, where leaders assign tasks based on age rather than skill. This may involve presuming that younger employees are automatically more tech-savvy or that older employees are less capable of adapting to change, which can limit opportunities and reinforce stereotypes.

Another form of feedback friction is when leaders avoid giving constructive feedback to older team members out of fear of offending them, while also walking on eggshells around Gen Z employees, assuming they are too sensitive. These hesitations prevent honest dialogue and hinder professional growth.

Promotion hesitancy is a form of bias. Some leaders follow unspoken rules about how long someone must stay at an organization before they are considered ready for leadership. This mindset often puts younger, high-performing employees at a disadvantage because they might be ready to lead but are overlooked due to their perceived lack of experience.

Finally, dismissive language can create cultural gaps and weaken trust. Phrases like "kids these days" or "old-school thinking" undermine contributions through generational stereotypes. When leaders use this language, even casually, they promote exclusion and restrict the psychological safety essential for collaboration across different age groups.

Leaders need to reflect on their own generational perspective and ask, "What assumptions am I making about people based on their generation?" Whether these assumptions involve loyalty, adaptability, or work ethic, they must be addressed. The most effective teams are guided by leaders who respond to behavior rather than bias.

Unchecked generational bias fragments teams and erodes psychological safety. It keeps people performing under a silent ceiling shaped not by skill but by generational assumptions.

How Leaders Can Check Their Generational Bias

Leaders can start addressing their generational bias by first recognizing it. This begins with reflection. Consider the assumptions or stories you tell yourself about each generation. Write them down and question where these beliefs originated. Were they taught to you? Inherited through culture or upbringing? Or molded by a challenging experience that led to a broad conclusion? Awareness is the initial step toward making a change.

The next step is to review your actions. Look at who you choose to mentor, who you regularly ask for input from, and who you consider for promotion. Notice any patterns. Are you unknowingly favoring people of a certain generation? Are your assumptions about someone's digital skills or adaptability based on facts or influenced by generation-related stereotypes?

Once you become aware, intentionally interrupt bias as it occurs. When a thought like, "she's probably not ready because she's just out of school," comes up, pause and examine it. Ask yourself, "What actual evidence do I have about her readiness?" Shift your focus to skills, data, and performance rather than assumptions tied to demographics.

Adopt a mindset of curiosity rather than criticism. Each generation brings its own values and perspectives shaped by the historical moments that influenced them. When someone's approach feels unfamiliar, resist the urge to judge and instead ask questions. Strive to understand their why before forming conclusions.

Establishing intergenerational learning opportunities can also reduce silos and foster empathy. When people with different experiences work side by side, they begin to see one another beyond generational shortcuts. Cross-functional projects and shared problem-solving allow experience and fresh perspective to meet in real time. In these settings, insight flows both ways. Some contribute context shaped by time and exposure, while others bring curiosity, adaptability, and emerging ways of thinking. The result is not hierarchy, but mutual respect built through collaboration.

Normalize conversations about generational experiences in the workplace. Promote open dialogue about how a person's upbringing and generational background influence their expectations and communication style. These discussions not only enhance mutual understanding but also foster opportunities for creative problem-solving and connection.

When generational conflict occurs, leaders should guide the conversation instead of trying to control it. This might sound like, "It seems like you're both approaching this project from different angles. Let's talk about what each of you values and find some common ground." That simple act of mediation helps team members feel heard and cuts down on defensiveness. It turns the conflict into a coaching opportunity rather than a silent standoff.

Sometimes, the root of generational conflict is not behavior, but emotion, feeling dismissed, irrelevant, or misunderstood. Leaders must be attuned to these emotional undercurrents and follow up with empathy. A younger employee labeled as too eager may simply be passionate. An older employee seen as resistant may just feel overlooked. Leaders hold themselves accountable by asking deeper questions, listening carefully, and repairing harm when needed.

And just like cauliflower, sometimes people need to be "prepared" differently. A team member who seems rigid might soften when they feel seen. A younger employee who appears disengaged may thrive with a mentor. Leadership involves adjusting the heat, seasoning the environment, and trusting that change is possible with the right attention and care.

Ultimately, the goal is not to eliminate generational differences but to lead through them. To make space at the table for everyone's voice and find ways to honor both tradition and change. A multi-generational team, when guided with intention, isn't a problem to solve. It is a dish that, when thoughtfully prepared, nourishes the entire organization with strength, balance, and depth.

Generational Intelligence

A Leadership Skill for Organizational Health

Generational intelligence is now essential for effective leadership. It is a crucial skill that helps leaders understand, connect with, and respond to the needs of a diverse, multigenerational workforce. Essentially, generational intelligence is the ability to recognize how different life experiences, cultural influences, and societal changes shape the values, motivations, and communication styles of people across various age groups. More importantly, it involves applying understanding with empathy, flexibility, and purpose.

Leadership today isn't about managing sameness. It's about fostering difference in a way that supports the organization's collective health and purpose. Leaders with high generational intelligence do more than just recognize that diversity exists. They leverage it to build stronger, more resilient teams. They know how to adapt their approach without losing clarity. They listen without judgment, communicate effectively across styles, and create an environment where people of all backgrounds feel seen and respected.

This skill becomes especially crucial for maintaining organizational health and well-being. Different generations experience and express well-being in unique ways. One team member might value stability and long-term security, while another might prioritize flexibility and purpose. Some may seek mentorship, transparency, or community. Generational intelligence enables leaders to address these needs without making assumptions or dismissing perspectives that differ from their own.

When leaders demonstrate generational intelligence, they:

- Strengthen psychological safety by honoring different communication and feedback styles
- Foster employee engagement by aligning purpose and values across roles
- Minimize workplace conflict by resolving misunderstandings early
- Foster better collaboration by promoting curiosity rather than criticism
- Develop inclusive frameworks that respond to changing workforce needs
- Encourage long-term retention by recognizing and supporting employees at every stage of their lives

Organizational well-being depends on more than just policies or perks. It requires leaders who are emotionally aware, relationally agile, and committed to understanding the people they lead. Generational intelligence isn't about labeling individuals; it's about building connections between them.

When leaders nurture this skill, they create workplaces that are not only more respectful but also more human. These are environments where trust develops, participation improves, and culture becomes a shared commitment rather than just a scripted message.

Generational intelligence exemplifies leadership in action. It is the way we maintain health, respect differences, and lead by creating space for everyone.

Chapter 8
Listening Through Friction
Turning Tension into Understanding with Intentional Listening

Conflict is noisy. It appears with raised eyebrows, long pauses, sharp words, or cold silence. As a leader, your instinct might be to defend, deflect, or disengage. Beneath all that tension is something simple, often ignored, a need to be heard. Listening through conflict means staying present, not just to what's being said but to the emotion behind it. It's a bold choice to lean in when your ego wants to pull back. It's not just hearing words; it's understanding the meaning behind the chaos. True listening isn't passive. It's active and deliberate. It requires you to quiet your internal defenses and make space for someone else's reality, even if that reality feels uncomfortable.

Understanding someone else's reality is one of the most vital skills a leader can develop. It serves as the foundation of empathy, emotional maturity, and inclusive leadership. Without it, leaders operate within an echo chamber, filtering others' experiences through their own biases, assumptions, and preferences. When leaders choose to understand someone else's reality, they foster deeper trust, improve communication, and make more ethical decisions. It's not about agreeing with that reality or fully relating to it; it's about recognizing that it *exists* and has meaning for the person living it.

The Power of Motivation

Why Understanding What Drives Employees Matters

When a leader takes the time to understand someone else's reality, they communicate that the person matters, that their experience carries weight, and that it will be respected. This fosters psychological safety, which is the foundation for high performance, creativity, and open feedback. It also helps leaders make better informed decisions. A policy that looks good on paper might unintentionally exclude or burden someone in practice. By understanding how people experience the workplace through their background, generation, race, family obligations, mental health, or lived trauma, a leader becomes better prepared to lead fairly and compassionately.

Understanding someone else's reality also helps prevent harmful assumptions. It's easy to label someone as disengaged, resistant, or unqualified when you don't see the full story. Maybe they're a single parent managing unseen challenges. Maybe they're new to the organization's culture and unsure how to speak up. Maybe they need time to process before replying. When you understand the reasons behind their actions, you can respond with strategy instead of judgment.

At the heart of every successful organization is a simple truth: people want to feel valued, recognized, and inspired by the work they do. As leaders, one of the most powerful actions we can take is to make an effort to understand what motivates our employees. When we understand what drives the individuals on our teams, we can connect their purpose to the organization's goals. This alignment not only boosts participation but also builds trust, loyalty, and long-term commitment.

Motivation isn't a one-size-fits-all. For some, it means growth and progress. For others, it might be stability, recognition, autonomy, or making a meaningful impact. When leaders don't explore these motivators, they risk making assumptions instead of understanding. And when employees feel misunderstood or overlooked, their engagement drops.

The impact of exploring employee motivation is extensive. It directly boosts engagement. Engaged employees are more productive, collaborative, and more committed to their teams' success. Engagement enhances job satisfaction. And satisfied employees are more inclined to contribute positively to their work environment.

Job satisfaction is a key indicator of organizational health. When employees feel fulfilled at work, they bring positive energy to every interaction. They approach problems more creatively, support their colleagues more generously, and handle stress with greater resilience. Conversely, dissatisfaction leads to frustration, withdrawal, and behaviors that weaken collaboration and trust.

An optimized culture starts with satisfied employees. When the workplace culture is healthy, participation becomes voluntary and enthusiastic. People don't just comply; they contribute. They take ownership, speak up, and show up with purpose.

And the effects are measurable. Optimized participation results in stronger business outcomes. Sales grow. Learning results improve. The bottom line gets stronger. Culture and participation are interconnected; they are closely linked.

Employee satisfaction does more than boost morale; it also shields the organization from internal toxicity. When employees are satisfied, they are less likely to participate in negative behaviors. Gossip, territorialism, disengagement, and resistance diminish when people feel connected to something that matters to them.

Leaders who take the time to understand what motivates their team are not just fostering relationships; they are laying the groundwork for a sustainable, high-performing organization.

Because when employees are motivated and satisfied, everyone benefits.

Leading Through Listening

Turning Insight into Impact

One of the most effective ways leaders can start understanding someone else's reality is by practicing insightful listening. This involves not just listening for answers or solutions but listening for meaning. When someone speaks, give them your full attention. Do not plan your response while they're talking; instead, focus on their tone, energy, and body language. Ask clarifying questions to show your engagement and to make sure you're hearing them correctly. Then, repeat what you've understood. For example, saying, "It sounds like you're saying X, is that accurate?" helps the speaker feel heard and allows you to check your interpretation. This kind of intentional listening builds trust and creates space for deeper conversations.

Another important skill is asking perspective-building questions. These go beyond the standard "How are you?" or "How's the project going?" and instead encourage genuine dialogue. Try asking, "What's something about your experience here I might not see?" or "Is anything making your work harder right now that I might not be aware of?" or even "What does support look like for you in moments of stress?" These questions send a clear signal that you are curious, not just checking a box. They invite honesty and recognize that there's more to someone's work life than what is visible on the surface.

Great leaders also take the time to understand their team members' backgrounds, not just their job roles. This means recognizing what motivates someone, what they value, what pressures they might be facing, and what kind of environment helps them perform their best. Even a brief, intentional conversation can reveal meaningful insights about how to support them more effectively. People are more than their output, and when a leader acknowledges the bigger picture, they become more connected and capable in their support.

Creating space for identity and lived experience is also essential. Encourage your team to bring their full selves to work, not just their title or job description. Make room for people to share their cultural backgrounds, personal histories, or perspectives if they choose to. Recognize how these identities influence the way they engage, communicate, and handle challenges. This is especially crucial when leading individuals from marginalized groups whose experiences might often be overlooked or misunderstood. Providing space to honor these realities foster belonging and allows everyone to be seen for who they truly are.

In structured settings like one-on-ones or team development sessions, a tool such as story-sharing exercises can help bring these perspectives to life. Ask team members to walk you through a typical day or to share a time when they felt unseen or unsupported. Use story-sharing to consider what they may be thinking, feeling, hearing, and experiencing. This exercise shifts the focus from productivity to humanity, offering valuable insight into how to lead with greater awareness.

At the same time, leaders must regularly examine their own internal filters. Every reaction, assumption, and decision is influenced by a personal lens shaped by one's upbringing, culture, privileges, and experiences. Ask yourself often, "Am I interpreting this situation through my perspective, or through theirs?" And when strong reactions occur, pause and consider, "What else might be true here?" This act of self-reflection creates space for growth and reminds you that your truth is not the only truth. Humility becomes the key to deeper understanding.

Finally, listening without taking action is empty. If you spend time understanding someone's reality but don't adjust your leadership, your effort becomes superficial. Show that you've heard them by modifying your coaching, communication style, and policies. If someone works better with written instructions rather than verbal guidance, make the change. If someone often feels left out in meetings, find ways to include their voice. When your actions mirror the insights you've gained, trust grows and the relationship becomes stronger. This is where true leadership exists, not just in what you hear, but in how you respond.

Some insights might challenge your preferences or seem unfamiliar, like cauliflower at a dinner where you expected comfort food. You don't have to love the taste to recognize its value. The more curious you are about how others see the world, the better equipped you are to guide them through it. Just like cauliflower, every person offers something nourishing, even if it's not what you would have chosen for yourself. When you lead with curiosity, you learn to recognize value without requiring familiarity or comfort.

At its core, listening through friction means that when the temperature rises and the room becomes tense, you don't shut down. You stay open. You observe your own triggers and choose not to be driven by them. You listen with curiosity instead of judgment. You listen to understand, not to win. This doesn't mean agreeing. It doesn't mean fixing. It means honoring that something real is trying to surface, and that realness deserves a place at the table. When tension appears, leaders must make a choice: escalate it, suppress it, or transform it. Transformation begins with naming the energy in the room. Say what others are sensing. A simple acknowledgment like "I can feel some tension here; let's pause for a moment" can neutralize power dynamics and open the floor for honesty. Then, breathe before you speak. One deep breath between hearing and responding creates space for thought instead of reactivity. Leaders who regulate themselves help regulate the room.

Instead of reacting with assumptions, ask open-ended questions like "Can you tell me more about what's coming up for you?" or "What would support look like for you right now?" These kinds of questions shift the conversation from defensive to reflective. Mirror back what you heard to ensure understanding: "What I'm hearing is that you felt dismissed in that meeting. Is that right?" This confirms comprehension without conceding agreement. Above all, stay in the moment, even if it's uncomfortable. Don't cut off emotion. Let people express frustration or disappointment. You don't have to fix it. Just witness it. That alone can diffuse defensiveness.

Empathy isn't about rescuing; it's about recognizing. It's the ability to step into someone else's world and feel with them, not for them. Empathetic leadership involves pausing to understand before offering solutions. It means creating space for emotions without judgment. It requires considering how decisions impact others emotionally, not just operationally. Leading with context, not just content, is key, and always remembering there's a story behind every performance.

To foster empathy, leaders should begin by slowing their decision-making and considering who will be impacted and how they might experience the outcome. During feedback, they can pause to reflect on what others may be thinking, feeling, worried about, or hoping for. Walking the floor, both literally and figuratively, helps leaders stay connected. It is through hallway conversations and informal interactions that trust develops. Most importantly, empathy grows when leaders demonstrate their humanity. When you show vulnerability, you create space for others to do the same.

The Importance of Curiosity in Leadership

Curiosity is one of the most overlooked leadership qualities, yet it has the power to change how a leader understands, engages, and guides others. Essentially, curiosity is the willingness to explore without judgment. It encourages leaders to stay open to what they don't yet know, ask thoughtful questions instead of making assumptions, and respond with inquiry rather than defensiveness. When a leader approaches their team, their work, and even conflict with curiosity, they shift the culture from one of certainty to one of learning.

Curiosity is active, not passive. It demands energy and intention. It resembles a leader who asks, "Tell me more about how you arrived at that decision," instead of rushing to correct someone. It appears in one-on-one meetings where the leader poses questions like, "What's something I might not see from my position?" or "What would make you feel more supported in your role?" Curiosity enables a leader to look beyond surface behavior. When someone is underperforming, curiosity asks, "What's getting in the way?" rather than assuming laziness or lack of motivation. When someone is difficult to work with, curiosity wonders, "What story are they carrying that might explain this?"

A curious leader gathers information before making decisions. They seek input, appreciate diverse perspectives, and genuinely aim to understand how their choices affect others. This not only fosters trust but also improves the quality of decision-making. When curiosity exists, people feel recognized. They feel safe to speak up, share ideas, admit struggles, and be themselves without fear of misunderstanding. Teams led by curious leaders tend to innovate more, collaborate more deeply, and recover faster from setbacks because they are grounded in psychological safety.

For the leader, curiosity becomes a powerful tool for resilience. It helps interrupt emotional reactivity. When tension rises, curiosity becomes the inner voice that says, "What else might be going on here?" rather than clinging to being right. It offers the leader a chance to grow, to stretch into new perspectives, and to lead not just with expertise but with humility. Curious leaders are learners. And learners adapt, evolve, and sustain influence in ways that command-and-control leadership never will.

Curiosity also helps us come to peace with what we may never fully understand. Some people will always be your cauliflower. You might not enjoy their style. You might not connect with their energy. You might not even understand why they do what they do. But curiosity provides another way in. You don't have to love cauliflower to be curious about how it nourishes others, how it takes on new flavors when prepared differently, or why it appears on so many tables even if it's not your favorite. The same is true in leadership. You don't have to feel personal affinity to be open-hearted. You don't have to enjoy every personality to ask thoughtful questions. Curiosity is how we bridge the gap between difference and dignity. It is how we lead with wonder, not walls.

When Empathy Is Missing

When empathy is absent, the damage becomes clear. High turnover often results. People don't leave their jobs; they leave leaders who make them feel invisible. Trust begins to break down. Teams stop communicating honestly and start performing just for safety rather than success. Collaboration becomes superficial, transactional, and guarded. The workplace may keep running, but it doesn't flourish.

Still, let's acknowledge a truth: not every leader feels naturally empathetic. And sometimes the person you're struggling to empathize with is your cauliflower. They rub you the wrong way, challenge your values, or drain your energy. What then? If empathy doesn't come easily, start by recognizing the gap. Say to yourself, "I'm finding it difficult to connect with this person. Why is that?" Awareness is the first step toward integrity. Then, focus on respect, not rapport. Even without emotional connection, you can act in ways that are respectful, fair, and professional. Empathy isn't just a feeling; it is a practice.

Use tools when instincts fall short. Lean into structured feedback frameworks and intentional check-ins. These serve as guideposts when emotions are unclear. Seek outside perspective. Ask someone who connects with that person for insight. "How do you experience them? What motivates them?" Borrow their lens if yours is clouded. And most powerfully, check the mirror. Sometimes the people we struggle with most are reflections of parts of ourselves we haven't made peace with. Ask yourself what this person reveals about you.

Lastly, don't fake it. Ground it. You don't have to pretend to like them, but you must lead them with dignity. Empathy can manifest as structure, fairness, and consistency even when chemistry is lacking. Some people are like cauliflower, nutrient dense, complex, and just not to your taste. That doesn't mean they don't belong on the plate. Leadership isn't about favoring your preferences. It's about creating a table where differences are respected, tension is explored, and listening becomes your most powerful seasoning.

What "If" Thinking

A Non-Negotiable Practice for Conscious Leadership

There is remarkable power in a question as simple as "What if?" For leaders, this question is not a sign of doubt but a signal of courage. It opens space for possibility without abandoning direction. When a leader asks, "What if?" they are not stepping away from decisiveness. They are creating room for insight, empathy, and broader understanding.

"What if?" invites pause before reaction, reflection before assumption, and imagination before repetition. In a world that rewards speed and certainty, the willingness to wonder becomes a quiet but radical leadership act.

What if the employee who seems disengaged is actually overwhelmed by unseen grief? What if the conflict between generations isn't about resistance but about a deep desire to be understood? What if your harshest critic is reflecting a part of yourself you've been unwilling to face? These questions don't weaken your leadership. They make it more human. They pull you out of vertical thinking , the kind that seeks control, authority, and hierarchy, and ground you in horizontal thinking, where relationships, stories, and context influence every decision. Horizontal thinking says, "Before I act, I will listen. Before I assume, I will ask. Before I conclude, I will consider what I do not yet know."

Throughout this book, we have explored themes that require this kind of reframing. From leading across generations to building respect without rapport, from facing conflict with dignity to understanding the impact of our own expectations, each moment provides an opportunity to pause and reflect. "What if I am wrong about them?" "What if I am wrong about me?" "What if the discomfort I feel is growth trying to speak?" These questions are not about self-doubt; they are about self-awareness. They keep us connected to empathy. They slow us down just enough to respond rather than react.

Practicing this mindset takes time. It requires reflection and the humility to admit we haven't arrived, along with the wisdom to understand we never fully will. Leaders who embrace "What if?" are not indecisive; they are deeply intentional. They recognize that every decision made with thoughtfulness, curiosity, and care becomes an act of alignment with their values. These leaders are not driven by fear or ego but by vision and a grounded understanding of who they are and who they are becoming. That kind of leadership doesn't just create better workplaces, it cultivates braver, kinder, and more connected people.

Understanding someone else's reality as a leader is not just a one-time act. It is a daily choice, a conscious effort to stay open when it would be easier to shut down, to remain curious when it would be easier to assume, and to lean in to listen when part of you wants to move on. Curiosity becomes the key to empathy. It encourages you to wonder instead of judge, to explore instead of retreat. It is the consistent force that helps you choose presence over performance, humility over ego, and relationship over control. When leaders lead with curiosity, they create environments where people feel truly known, not just managed, and seen, not just evaluated.

Some realities will never feel familiar to you. They may challenge your instincts, stretch your understanding, or leave you feeling unsure. They might be your version of cauliflower, something you don't naturally enjoy but still recognize has value. You don't have to like it to be curious about why others do. The same goes for people. Curiosity allows you to lead with respect, even when connection isn't immediate. You don't have to enjoy someone's communication style, share their worldview, or feel a natural connection to lead them with empathy, respect, and integrity. Leadership isn't about forcing a taste for everything. It's about asking questions that bring clarity to what you don't yet understand. It's about creating space at the table for people and perspectives that may never match your flavor but still matter. Because honoring someone's reality isn't about your comfort; it's about your courage to lead with curiosity and their right to belong.

Chapter 9
Refusing to Perform
A New Kind of Leadership

For too long, leadership has been viewed as a performance. We've been told to appear polished, project confidence, and use executive presence. Smile even when it weighs heavy. Soften your voice. Don't take things personally. Don't let them see your doubt. Don't let them see you sweat. Certainly, never let them see you cry. The job description never stated you had to be a *performer,* but we all received the message.

Leadership shifted into acting a role, becoming who people needed you to be rather than showing who you actually were. The better you mastered the act, the farther you advanced. You were praised for your ability to adapt, endure, absorb, and push through obstacles. For blending in while standing out. For smiling through betrayal. For not taking things personally, even when they struck a deeply personal chord.

But performance is not leadership. And leadership cannot be fully optimized through performance alone. When you lead from a version of yourself that is curated rather than true, there will always be unrealized potential left on the table, for you and for the organization. What brought you here may earn approval, but it will never allow you to become the leader you were meant to be.

There is a kind of leadership that refuses to perform. It does not shrink away from discomfort. It does not contort itself to be palatable. It does not mask the truth with strategy. It is grounded in alignment rather than approval. Refusing to perform is not about abandoning professionalism. It is about honoring yourself. It is about leading with your values visible. It is about saying the thing that needs to be said, not the thing that will earn applause. It is about prioritizing clarity over charisma. Purpose over popularity. Authenticity is not just a leadership trend. It's not merely a survival skill either. It is a human-centered, heart-driven quality that should be at the core of every leader's growth. It invites reflection, self-awareness, and the courage to lead from within. Leaders who embrace authenticity as a guiding principle create spaces where trust grows, people thrive, and leadership becomes a force for connection rather than control.

When you lead from a place of performance, you spend your energy managing perception. You become an actor in your own life. You speak carefully rather than truthfully. You use your voice but not your heart. Eventually, you lose track of which version of yourself you're bringing into the room.

When you lead with authenticity, you conserve your energy for what truly matters. You align your actions with your values. You stop wasting energy on pretending. You make decisions you can live with. You build confidence not from applause, but from congruence. You find peace not in perfection, but in alignment.

This type of leadership is not always easy. It may not always be celebrated. Some might say it's too much, too emotional, too sensitive, too principled. Others will tell you that your expectations are too high. But if being yourself disqualifies you from a table, then that table was never meant for you in the first place.

Authentic leadership is a different kind of power. It isn't about the loudest voice in the room or the title on the door. It's the power to choose yourself before seeking approval. It's the power to break cycles of harm by refusing to participate in them. It's the power to create culture instead of conforming to one that doesn't align with your values. At its highest, authentic leadership is leadership rooted in heart. And heart is not a weakness. Heart is the courage to immerse yourself in your truth so deeply that you can offer your full self, honest, vulnerable, and consistent, to the people you lead.

Leading with heart means showing up as the same person in every setting. It involves leading from alignment instead of performance. It means letting your values guide your choices rather than fear or what's popular. This kind of leadership creates space for others to breathe, trust, and bring their own strengths and perspectives forward. Giving your authentic self to those you lead truly matters. It matters because people can tell when leadership is genuine. Trust isn't built on image; it's built on presence. When your team sees your integrity and consistency, they respond with greater engagement, stronger commitment, and deeper ownership of their work.

Authentic leadership sees people not as resources, but as individuals with unique value and purpose. It appreciates their contributions, growth, and goals. It fosters a culture where communication is open, accountability is shared, and connection is purposeful. But what does intentional connection really mean?

At its core, connection involves recognizing and respecting each person as an individual with their own story and perspective. It's not about superficial check-ins or knowing just a few facts about someone's role or life. Instead, it's about building relationships based on understanding, trust, and care. Leadership rooted in connection understands that people are not defined solely by their productivity. They are shaped by their stories, values, and sense of purpose in their work and beyond.

To connect is to be curious. It involves asking questions not only about job performance but also about what motivates individuals. It means understanding what success looks like to them, both personally and professionally. For one person, success might mean financial stability and providing for their family. For another, it might mean creative freedom, skill development, or the chance to lead. Connection enables a leader to recognize these differences and respond appropriately. Genuine connection also requires knowing what matters to someone outside of their daily tasks. What are their long-term goals? What are they proud of? What challenges are they silently facing? What helps them feel supported, not just managed?

Connection takes time. Genuine connection can't be rushed because each person is at their own stage when it comes to trust. Some people will open up quickly, while others need more time, more consistency, and more proof that it's safe to be vulnerable. Leaders must understand this. Building real connection through leadership requires presence, patience, and persistence.

It means showing up consistently, listening intently, and following through on what you hear. It means valuing a person's well-being just as much as their results. And it is not something you do occasionally, leaders must demonstrate this every single time, with every member of their team. Connection is not a one-time achievement. It is a practice, and it lives in the rhythm of how you lead.

One of the best ways to build this rhythm is through weekly one-on-ones. These aren't just meetings; they are chances to form genuine connections, understand how your people are doing, and create space for honesty. If you aren't holding regular one-on-ones with your team, you're missing out on one of the most valuable opportunities to build trust, connection, and alignment.

Connection isn't about crossing personal boundaries or becoming too involved. It's about seeing people as a whole, recognizing their strengths, understanding their background, and respecting the experiences that shaped them. When employees feel recognized in this way, something powerful happens: engagement increases, loyalty develops, and trust becomes a mutual exchange.

A connected leader is not only more informed, but also more impactful. When people feel genuinely known, they are more willing to contribute fully. They bring more of their ideas, energy, and creativity to the table. They take ownership because they feel invested. Connection is not a leadership accessory; it is the foundation of a healthy, people-centered culture. It builds the kind of team where individuals are empowered, differences are respected, and collective success is driven by personal alignment.

When you take the time to genuinely understand the people you lead, you foster more than just efficiency. You foster a sense of belonging. And belonging isn't created through authority or position; it's built through participation.

When leaders choose to build relationships instead of relying on hierarchy, and when they intentionally create space for people's ideas, concerns, and aspirations, they foster the conditions for a healthy, connected organization. This is where trust develops. This is where people feel seen, heard, and valued, not just for what they do, but for who they are.

And when that trust establishes itself, something powerful begins to occur. Respect deepens. Clarity becomes sharper. Commitment turns into a shared value rather than something imposed. In cultures like this, people feel psychologically safe. They contribute more openly, collaborate more efficiently, and bring increased creativity to their work. They stay because the environment reflects who they are and who they aspire to become.

The organization shifts from being just a workplace to a place where people can thrive. This is the legacy of genuine leadership. It's not only about hitting targets but about building cultures of trust. It's not just about creating systems but about improving how people experience work every single day. Leading with heart means leading in a way that empowers others rather than diminishes them. When people are strong, aligned, and engaged, the organization benefits as well.

Refusing to perform is a risk. It means expressing your truth. It involves being misunderstood. It requires standing firm when it would be easier to smooth things over. But it also brings freedom. It means returning to yourself. It entails leading from a place of grounded integrity. It allows you to look in the mirror at the end of the day and say, I led in alignment with who I am. Let's be honest about something leaders rarely admit aloud: most organizations still reward performance over authenticity. We are told to bring our whole selves to work, but only if that self fits the mold. Be authentic, but not too emotional. Be honest, but not disruptive. Be confident but not intimidating. Be collaborative, but still competitive. These mixed messages are exhausting. And for many leaders, they create a quiet but relentless tension: How do I succeed here without becoming someone I'm not?

What makes this even more challenging is that we don't always recognize exhaustion for what it truly is. Performance fatigue can masquerade as anxiety, depression, loneliness, or a persistent sense of dread when facing the workday. It might appear as frustration, disengagement, or even apathy. Leaders are not immune to this, nor are their teams. The burden of performing rather than participating weighs on everyone. That's why it's crucial for leaders to identify these signals, not only in themselves but also in those they lead. Only then can we view our teams as whole, with the awareness and empathy necessary to lead in a way that restores connection rather than depletes it.

The truth is, many workplaces still perpetuate the illusion that advancing requires performance. That you must adapt, accommodate, and bend until you embody a certain perception of leadership. One that is often outdated, sanitized, and impossible to sustain without personal sacrifice.

This belief is not only harmful but also unsustainable.

Here is what happens when we lead from performance instead of authenticity: we burn out. We disengage. We start to resent the work. We lose our sense of meaning. We experience physical and emotional fatigue. The pressure to suppress parts of who we are is not just an emotional burden, it can become a health issue. Chronic stress, anxiety, sleep disruption, migraines, high blood pressure, digestive problems, all are real consequences of the cognitive dissonance between who we are and who we pretend to be. Performance might earn you the title, the office, the bigger paycheck, but at what cost?

Sustainability in leadership, true long-term sustainability, relies on authenticity. Not only for your health but also for your productivity, engagement, your team's trust, and your sense of peace. When you lead from alignment, you aren't constantly managing a version of yourself. You show up with clarity and consistency. You make decisions more quickly because you aren’t navigating a thousand invisible filters. You connect more deeply. You recover from conflict faster. You become more resilient, not because you endure more, but because you’re no longer performing your strength. You’re living in it.

Authenticity doesn't mean saying everything that comes to mind. It doesn't mean giving up discretion or professionalism. It involves making space for your true self to guide your leadership. It means letting your values, not fears, shape your decisions. It means honoring your voice instead of rehearsing what you think will be most acceptable. You can climb without erasing yourself. You can succeed and still sleep peacefully. But it requires challenging the myth that performance is the only way to rise. This is the new kind of leadership: one grounded in truth.

Leadership does ask for flexibility. It calls us to listen, adapt, and evolve. But there is a meaningful difference between being flexible and being asked to conform to a set of standards that disconnects you from your guiding principles. If you feel your voice being silenced, your style constantly questioned, or your presence minimized in order to fit in, that is something to notice. That noticing is not a weakness. It is clarity. It is the moment where you pause and ask yourself, is this version of leadership mine, or is it something I've been told I have to become? Can I keep growing in this space without compromising who I am? This is not a rejection of growth or structure. It is an invitation to reflect. To choose alignment over approval. To make space for your full self as you continue the work of leading.

You don't need to leave parts of yourself behind to lead. You don't have to perform to succeed. It's okay to grow and remain true to yourself. If your environment constantly requires you to change who you are, that might be a sign to reconsider not your ability, but your surroundings. You can succeed without sacrificing your identity. You can lead without losing your voice. And you can belong in a way that strengthens who you are, not erases it.

The truth is, some leaders are performing without even realizing it. I didn't. I wasn't aware that I had been performing until anxiety and discontentment quietly crept in, disrupting my peace in ways I couldn't immediately identify. It wasn't until I allowed myself to sit with that discomfort and fully explore its source that I recognized it for what it was. I wasn't being true to myself or my leadership style. I was leading based on what I thought was expected of me, rather than who I truly was. For those of us who find our identity in our careers, this is a humbling realization. It forces a reckoning. A change is necessary, not just in how we lead, but in how we see ourselves.

Chapter 10
The Power of Being Relatable

People want to follow someone they can relate to, not just someone they admire from a distance.

In a world overwhelmed by image management and performative jargon, authentic leaders stand out as a breath of fresh air. They feel real. Grounded. Approachable. Human. And through that humanity, there is strength. Because when people can relate to you, they trust you. And when they trust you, they listen, follow, and grow under your leadership.

Relatability isn't about oversharing or becoming everyone's best friend. It's about revealing who you are behind the role. It's about showing vulnerability when needed and leading with both strength and softness.

It means being honest even when you don't have all the answers. It means listening rather than reacting. It means sharing your thought process instead of pretending to be certain. It means admitting when something is difficult instead of pretending it is easy. It means showing compassion before offering correction. It means making room for laughter, struggle, and humanity in your team, not as distractions, but as signs of a healthy workplace.

Being relatable helps build bridges.

It encourages others to be authentic. It fosters psychological safety. It improves team culture. But being relatable alone isn't enough. When you combine relatability with credibility and care, you create a leadership style that earns respect and leaves a lasting impression.

Credibility is built through consistency, by making decisions that align with your words and values. It appears in the way you carry yourself. Credibility isn't just a title; it's evidence of your integrity in action.

Care is shown in the small, intentional ways you connect with others. It exists in how you listen, how you follow up, and how you think about the impact of your words. It appears in the moments when you hold space for others, even when you're tired, even when it would be easier to withdraw. Care reminds people that they matter beyond their output.

When you lead with all three, relatability, credibility, and care- you create a ripple effect that extends well beyond your job description. You build trust. You foster culture. You inspire belonging. And that is what people remember. Not how perfectly you presented, how polished your emails were, or how many buzzwords you knew. They remember the quality of your presence. They remember your honesty, your humanity, and your willingness to be real.

Ultimately, lasting leadership isn't about how it appears on paper. It's about how genuine it feels in practice. It's also about inspiring others to lead with integrity too. Because authenticity isn't just a gift you offer yourself.

It's a gift you extend to everyone around you.

When Authenticity Threatens the Room

Not everyone will praise your choice to lead with authenticity.

In fact, some leaders may feel very uncomfortable with it. Your presence, clarity, openness, values, and voice highlight the areas they have hidden behind performance. Without saying a word, your authenticity acts as a mirror. For leaders who have built their identity around image, control, or compliance, that reflection can feel intimidating.

They may question your motives.
They may call you too emotional or too idealistic.
They may accuse you of being unprofessional when

you point out what others ignore. They may try to undermine your credibility because they cannot match your clarity.

Sometimes it will be subtle. You may notice being excluded from important meetings. You may hear passive-aggressive comments. You may find your work minimized, your questions dismissed, or your tone picked apart.

Other times, it will be more direct. You might be labeled difficult, rebellious, or disruptive. Not because you are wrong, but because you are authentic.

This is when your leadership will be tested. This is when you must stay grounded in your values. You are not responsible for the insecurity of others. You are responsible for your integrity.

When this happens, respond with steadiness. Let your work speak. Let your consistency build trust. Let your empathy remain intact. You do not need to shrink to make someone else more comfortable. You do not need to match their energy. You do not need to explain away your authenticity.

Instead, stay grounded. Keep showing up with transparency. Keep making decisions that reflect your values. Keep being the leader who listens openly, speaks honestly, and acts intentionally.

Your credibility will grow. So will your influence. Not because you played the part, but because you stayed true. Genuine leadership isn't always the quickest way to be accepted. It is, however, the clearest path to earning respect.

When you encounter resistance, don't assume you're doing something wrong. It might mean you're challenging something that has long gone unquestioned. You won't always be the most agreeable voice in the room, but you can be the most trusted. And that kind of leadership creates a legacy.

Redefining Legacy

The Quiet Power of Staying the Course

Legacy is often seen as the sum of your career achievements, the titles you've held, the impact you've made, and the recognition you've received. While that is one form of legacy, it's not the only one. Legacy isn't just what you leave behind professionally; it also includes what you carry forward through your way of living.

There is a quieter kind of legacy, one that rarely makes headlines or fills résumés. It is the personal legacy that comes from living with conviction. It is the internal compass that guides your decisions, leadership, and relationships. It is shaped by your values, integrity, and your willingness to stay grounded in what matters most to you, even when the world around you shifts.

This kind of legacy is not always celebrated, but it is deeply felt. It is built in moments when you choose truth over approval. When you walk away from what is popular to stand firm with what is right. When you stay rooted in your own pillars of strength, grit, kindness, honesty, faith, and compassion, even when those around you question, resist, or try to wear you down.

There will be seasons when staying the course means walking alone. When your decisions may confuse others, disappoint some, or disrupt norms. But personal legacy isn't about popularity. It's about consistency. It's about honoring what you stand for, not just on your highlight reel, but in the quiet corners of your daily life.

Your legacy is reflected in how you treated others during difficult times. It's evident in the boundaries you maintained, the accountability you took, and the grace you showed, even when it wasn't acknowledged. It's expressed in how you showed up, not only for the significant moments but also for the ones no one noticed.

Legacy is more than just a career. It's a guiding compass. And if you've held onto yours, even through resistance or isolation, you've already created something worthwhile. Something lasting. Something that others will feel long after your name is no longer on the door.

Chapter 11
When Discomfort Becomes a Guide

Of all the leadership disciplines I have studied and practiced, the ability to sit with discomfort is the one I return to most often. Not because it is comfortable, but because it is where clarity is forged. Discomfort interrupts autopilot. It exposes misalignment, surfaces truth, and signals growth that cannot be reached through ease alone. While many leaders are taught to override discomfort, manage around it, or push through it in pursuit of results, the most effective leaders learn to listen to it. Discomfort is not a weakness in leadership. It is a form of internal intelligence. When acknowledged and engaged with intention, it becomes one of the most reliable guides a leader has.

Leadership Framework

How Leaders Use Discomfort as a Guide

Leaders who grow through discomfort do not treat it as a problem to eliminate. They treat it as information to interpret. This requires a disciplined internal practice built on three leadership behaviors.

The first is noticing. Effective leaders develop awareness of how discomfort shows up in the body and mind. Tightness in the chest, restlessness, fatigue, or irritation are not distractions. They are signals. Noticing means pausing long enough to recognize that something within you is responding before you react outwardly. Leaders who fail to honor discomfort often mistake urgency for importance and reaction for decisiveness.

The second is staying present. Once discomfort is noticed, leadership maturity requires staying with it rather than escaping it. This does not mean indulging emotion or becoming stuck. It means resisting the instinct to fix, distract, or override the feeling. Staying present allows the emotional charge to settle and the message beneath it to emerge. Leaders who stay present do not rush to action for relief. They allow insight to surface before making decisions.

The third is listening for meaning. Discomfort always carries information. It may be pointing to a boundary that has been crossed, a value that has been compromised, a truth that has been avoided, or growth that is required. Listening means asking what this discomfort is revealing about alignment, leadership identity, or direction. Leaders who listen to discomfort lead with clarity instead of control. They make decisions rooted in integrity rather than impulse.

Sitting With Discomfort

A Practice in Presence

I understand what it means to live in a constant state of urgency. For a long time, I moved through the world in fight-or-flight mode. I was constantly managing, and pushing forward. I was conditioned, maybe unintentionally, to avoid discomfort at all costs. Keep working. Keep walking. Keep talking. That was the rhythm I knew. My nervous system rarely relaxed. I had become so used to the pressure that I no longer saw it as pressure. Discomfort, to me, was not a sign to be acknowledged. It was something to be outrun.

I did not yet realize that discomfort has meaning. That it offers insight. That it is part of the story we live, whether we notice it or not. I had never been shown how to be still when facing unease. So I did what many of us do. I buried it. I ignored it. I filled every moment of my time and energy to avoid it. Until I couldn't anymore. Eventually, the weight of everything I had suppressed began to surface. I could feel it physically, emotionally, and spiritually. It became clear that I needed a different way of being. Among the many things I learned, one lesson stood out: how to sit with my uncomfortableness. Not escape it. Not fix it. Just sit with it. This was not easy.

At first, the stillness felt unbearable. The silence was deafening. The emotional ache was sharp and disorienting. But over time, something began to change. When I gave discomfort space to speak, it uncovered truths I had buried for years. My body started to relax. My thoughts softened. A quiet clarity emerged, one that had always been waiting beneath the surface.

I reached a point where overriding discomfort was no longer sustainable. The signals were consistent, physical, emotional, and cognitive. Instead of managing symptoms, I chose to pay attention to what my system was communicating. That choice required stillness, regulation, and a willingness to stay present with discomfort rather than push past it. The most valuable outcome was not a solution or protocol, but the ability to listen long enough to understand what the discomfort was asking of me.

I had become very skilled at ignoring my own discomfort. But now I was learning to face it with grace. I was discovering that stillness is not empty. It is filled with information. It reveals where we hurt, what we carry, and what we need to release. It teaches us that we are safe in our own presence, that we can hold pain without losing ourselves.

Discomfort does not announce itself intellectually. It registers in the body first.

There is physical weight to emotional discomfort. It settles in the chest, tightens the shoulders, and stirs the stomach. Sometimes it appears as restlessness, sometimes as fatigue. It can ache like something you cannot name. Discomfort tends to occupy space in both the body and the mind, pulling our attention inward and demanding to be felt, even when we would rather ignore it. Most of us are conditioned to avoid discomfort. We rush to fix, to numb, to distract. We scroll, schedule, and silence. But something sacred happens when we resist the urge to escape and instead choose to sit quietly with what unsettles us. Sitting with discomfort is not passive; it is one of the most courageous acts we can undertake. It means staying with the feeling long enough to understand it. Holding space for pain without rushing to solve it. Witnessing the internal stirrings that tell us something is misaligned, not as a problem to fix, but as a message to honor. This process hurts. It pulls us inward where the noise is loudest. It calls for patience, tenderness, and a kind of honesty most of us have been taught to avoid. But the longer we sit, the quieter things become. Not immediately, but eventually. The emotional intensity softens. The mental clutter begins to clear. And then, almost without warning, something shifts. A pathway forward appears. A truth surfaces. A decision becomes clearer.

Sitting with discomfort builds resilience in the deepest way. It teaches us that we can withstand pain without breaking, and that we can be uncomfortable without losing ourselves. It's not about suffering for its own sake; it's about listening to what discomfort is trying to teach us. Often, it shows us where we need to grow, what we need to release, or what we've been avoiding that must finally be faced. There's magic in this kind of stillness. Not the glittering kind, but the quiet kind that signals the start of real change. Discomfort is not the enemy; it's often the doorway. And when we learn to sit with it instead of running from it, we meet parts of ourselves we might never have encountered otherwise. The uncomfortable moments aren't signs that something is wrong; they're invitations to return to ourselves. They are essential, not optional, in the practice of self-discovery.

There is something truly empowering about being able to sit with discomfort and trust that you will find your way through it. Not by force, but through presence. Not by escaping, but by allowing. Over time, the heaviness lifts. The path becomes clear. And we return to ourselves, not in spite of the discomfort, but because we made space for it.

To sit with discomfort is simple and profoundly difficult. Find a comfortable place in a quiet, private setting. Close your eyes. Do not try to fix anything. Do not analyze. Simply notice. Notice what is happening in your body. Where do you feel tension? Where do you feel heaviness, restlessness, or heat? Pay attention to your breath without changing it. Notice the sounds around you. Notice the urge to move, to open your eyes, to escape the silence. Do not be surprised if the quiet feels sharp or if discomfort rises quickly. This is normal. Resist the impulse to interrupt the moment. Stay present. Let the sensations come and go without judgment. Sit long enough to feel what stirs within you. Discomfort does not need to be solved. It needs to be witnessed. And in that witnessing, something begins to loosen This is how you begin to hear what your body and inner voice have been trying to communicate.

This framework is not abstract. It is practical. Leaders who notice, stay present, and listen with greater steadiness. They regulate themselves before they regulate others. They pause rather than react. They build trust because they are anchored in self-awareness instead of performance.

Growth doesn't happen in comfort. It takes place during the stretch, the pause, and moments when we're unsure, unsettled, or searching. Complacency doesn't lead to success; it results in stagnation. But discomfort, if we're willing to sit with it, can act as a guide, a compass pointing us back to what truly matters, what is real, and ultimately, to ourselves. Sitting with discomfort is not separate from leadership; it is its foundation. Authentic, intentional participation in leadership begins with the willingness to look inward and confront what remains unsettled within us. This inner work encourages us to slow down, pay attention, and become aware of our emotions, beliefs, and assumptions before they quietly influence our leadership. When leaders engage fully and intentionally with their self-awareness, they lead more clearly, compassionately, and purposefully. They foster cultures of safety because they have learned how to feel safe in their own truth.

Leadership identity isn't determined solely by public presence or participation. It originates from the quiet choices we make away from the spotlight. How we manage discomfort privately shows our preparedness to hold space for others publicly. Leaders who have learned to stay present with their own uncertainty and pain are better able to create space for others to do the same. They don't lead from a performance mindset; they lead from participation, fully engaged, emotionally available, and grounded in authenticity.

This book embodies that belief. It's not advocating for perfect leadership but for intentional presence, leading from the inside out. It highlights that discomfort isn't something to avoid but something to embrace, learn from, and grow through. If discomfort is part of your story, as it is mine, may you find strength in staying present with it. And may that presence become the most powerful part of your leadership.

Chapter 12
The Impact You Choose

Impact is not just the result of leadership. It's a fundamental part of leadership identity. It shows not only what we do but how we do it and why. The way we show up, the presence we bring into a room, and the intent behind our decisions shape our impact more than any policy, process, or performance metric ever could.

As leaders, we are always leaving an imprint. Whether we realize it or not, our choices have far-reaching effects. Every conversation, decision, and reaction matters. That's why self-awareness and intention are crucial for effective leadership. When we understand our values and follow a well-defined leadership compass, we are more likely to lead in a way that reflects who we are and who we aspire to be.

Impact is maximized when it is aligned with purpose. To make a genuine, positive difference for individuals, teams, or the organization, leaders must be clear about their intent. Authenticity and intentionality are essential. They form the foundation for caring about the effect our decisions have on others. We have all seen leaders make choices without fully considering their impact. Whether driven by urgency, ego, or habit, such decisions can have lasting effects on morale, trust, and culture. Sometimes the consequences are immediate; other times, they emerge slowly through disengaged employees, fractured teams, or lost credibility. Leadership disconnected from impact tends to be reactive, while impact-driven leadership is transformative.

To lead intentionally, we must ask ourselves not just *what* we are doing but *also why*. Why this decision, and why now? Who might be impacted by this choice, and in what way? What values are guiding this action, and what message does it convey? The more deeply we explore and define our leadership values, the better we understand the kind of impact we aim to have. The leadership compass we carry helps us navigate complexity without losing sight of our purpose. It keeps us grounded when outcomes are uncertain. It reminds us that success is not only about what gets accomplished but also about who we become and how others are affected along the way.

Your leadership identity isn't just formed by your achievements. It's shaped by the impact you have on the people you encounter. When that impact is rooted in authenticity and guided by intention, it becomes something others feel, remember, and carry forward. If you're like me, you find deep fulfillment in knowing that your leadership has made a positive difference in others' lives. I love seeing the impact I've made by helping people grow, and I genuinely take pride in watching organizations thrive because of my contributions and authentic participation.

But this sense of impact is not only external. It also resides within us as a quiet feeling of connection, belonging, and a deep understanding that we have contributed something good and meaningful. This is why intentional impact is important. Authentic leadership isn’t just about reacting or showing up as we are; it’s about showing up intentionally. It requires purposeful awareness of the kind of impact we aim to make and how we want others to experience our leadership. Fully understanding this isn’t optional; it’s essential. Leading with clarity, compassion, and consistency depends on it. When we choose our impact thoughtfully, we lead in a way that supports others’ success while remaining true to ourselves.

Leadership is defined by the impact you choose to make each day. Not through grand gestures or executive summaries, but in how you navigate the everyday moments that reveal your values. It shows in the way you greet the person who feels invisible. It’s in how you hold space for grief, anger, or confusion without rushing to fix it. It’s in how you remember someone's name, their story, or the burden they silently carry. It's in how you own your mistakes, repair harm when it's done, and stay present when the air feels heavy with disappointment.

Leadership is not measured by how many emails you send, how many meetings you attend, or how flawless your slide deck appears. Those are simply functions of the job. They keep the engine running, but they are not the heartbeat. True leadership is found in the impact you leave on the people around you. It's felt in the moments when others breathe easier because you entered the room, not because you took control, but because you brought clarity, steadiness, and calm. It's whether people feel more courageous after speaking with you, not because you gave them all the answers, but because your presence reminded them, they already hold strength and wisdom. It's evident in how your leadership creates space for others to rise, not by dominating the room, but by making room for different voices, ideas, and talents to emerge.

Integrity isn't something you just talk about. It's something others experience through your decisions, consistency, tone, and your ability to align what you say with what you do. Credibility isn't handed to you; it's earned over time by how you show up, follow through, and handle pressure. Empathy isn't a soft skill; it's a powerful presence that makes others feel seen, valued, and understood. Your leadership compass, shaped by your values and principles, must stay steady even when circumstances try to pull you away from it. These are the markers of lasting leadership: not performance or perfection, but presence, integrity, and trust. When you lead with these, your leadership becomes more than a role; it becomes a legacy.

True leadership shows itself in moments often unnoticed. It's not during performance reviews or when applause is loud. It's in how you speak to someone who can't offer anything in return. It's in how you advocate for someone whose voice trembles. It's in the restraint you show when you're angry. It's in the accountability you take when no one would have blamed you for walking away. It appears in how you listen, not just to respond, but to understand. Not just to check a box, but to let someone know they matter. Leadership is about how you help others feel seen. Whether you slow down enough to notice exhaustion in someone's eyes. Whether you see when someone's voice goes quieter or their laughter fades, and whether you care enough to ask why. It's defined by how you pause to reflect instead of react. By choosing to respond intentionally rather than defensively. By the strength it takes to stay soft when everything inside urges you to harden. By the ability to choose clarity over control, connection over command, and truth over comfort. Most importantly, it's shown in how you show up when the room is tense and the conversation tough. When stakes are high, and your ego wants to protect itself. When accountability is needed and emotions run raw. Do you meet discomfort with grace and grit, or do you hide behind position and power? Do you lean into repair, or do you use silence and withdrawal as weapons? This is where the heart of leadership lies, in the spaces between what is visible and what is felt. In the courage to lead not for appearance but for integrity. Not to seek praise but to serve. Leadership that truly changes people isn't about seeking credit. It's about seeing the humanity in every room and daring to lead from that place.

I've chosen to be the type of leader who understands that the most important work often happens quietly, behind closed doors. The leader I strive to be isn't always visible. I don't always receive credit, but that's never the point. My advocacy doesn't come with a microphone; it shows up when no one else is in the room to defend the people I serve. I fight for what's fair and just, even when those I advocate for have no idea it's happening. I sit in rooms where decisions are made and ask the hard questions. I identify the gaps. I push back on systems that quietly devalue the humans within them. I do this not for recognition, but because I believe in leadership that uplifts.

I build systems that protect, elevate, and nourish employees, often before they've found the words to ask for what they need. I think about sustainability not just in terms of budgets and bottom lines, but in terms of energy, dignity, and mental wellness. I hold the tension between what the organization needs to survive and what the people inside it need to thrive. That balancing act is not always graceful. But it is intentional. It is rooted in care.

I champion other leaders, especially when they are not in the room to speak for themselves. I understand what it means to be misunderstood, misread, or overlooked. So, when I see someone doing the hard work with integrity, I acknowledge it. I elevate it. I will defend it. Because part of my leadership compass is to ensure that leadership is not just recognized when it's loud and visible, but also when it is steady, humble, and authentic. I speak up for the employee who is exhausted and questioning their place. I bring up issues that others are afraid to mention. I try to humanize policies and remind decision-makers that metrics are not more important than morale. That people matter. That culture is more than just a slogan.

And most of the time, the people I do this for never know.

They will not know the hours I spend rewriting policies to be more humane. They will not see the late-night reflections that drive my next tough conversation. They will not hear how I redirect bias or quietly protect someone's dignity in an HR meeting. They won't understand the weight I carry walking the fine line between empathy and accountability. But that's okay. Because leadership has never been about being seen. It's about responsibility.

I choose to be the kind of leader who leads with conscience, care, and intention. Who believes that every system we encounter either causes harm or helps to repair it, and I want to be on the side of repair. Even if no one sees it, even if no one knows. Because I see it, and because I know.

You hold more power than you realize. Not the kind that controls outcomes, but the kind that shapes experiences. The kind that creates safety. The kind that unlocks potential. With every conversation, question, and choice, you are defining your legacy. You are showing others what leadership looks like. Whether you mean to or not, you are setting the tone. And that tone resonates. It resonates in how your team takes risks. It resonates in how they talk about their work. It resonates in whether they feel they belong. When the noise fades, how are you using your influence to build something better and what quiet legacy are you leaving behind?

Throughout this book, we have examined authenticity, conflict, empathy, curiosity, bias, and belonging. We have expanded the traditional view of leadership to include more human qualities. You now see that leadership is not about perfection. It's about presence. It's not about being the smartest person in the room. It's about being the most grounded, the most accountable, and the most willing to grow. You have the opportunity to lead in a way that restores people instead of draining them. You can invite difference instead of fearing it. That creates space for reality instead of demanding performance.

You get to choose the kind of leader you want to be. Not just once, but every day. When you walk into a room. When you give feedback. When you mediate tension. When you listen to someone who sees the world differently. The impact isn't reserved for grand gestures; it's built into everyday actions. Like the decision to approach hard conversations with care. Or the willingness to stay curious instead of shutting down. Or the humility to repair what has been broken. The leaders who leave a lasting impact aren't the ones with all the answers; they are the ones committed to asking better questions.

And so, we return to the metaphor that has carried us through cauliflower. A simple vegetable that has become a symbol for everything we have unpacked. Cauliflower is not flashy. It is not everyone's favorite. But it is versatile. It absorbs what it is surrounded by. It holds its shape even when roasted by heat. It can be misunderstood or pushed aside, but when prepared with care, it reveals richness and nourishment. Leadership is much the same. It is quiet strength. It is adaptability. It is the ability to show up fully in moments of pressure and bring something of value to the table. The work you do each day may not always be seen, but it shapes the experience of everyone around you. You are not just creating the environment, you are part of what transforms it. And the people you lead are part of it too. Some will be easy to work with. Others will challenge your palate. But each one brings something essential. Your role is not to like every flavor. Your role is to respect the nourishment in each person's truth, to stay present in the heat, and to lead with enough curiosity and courage to create something meaningful together.

Let this serve as your lasting reminder: Your impact isn't defined by your title, perfection, or ability to please others. It's shaped quietly through moments where you honor your truth, lead with integrity, and live in alignment with what truly matters to you. You don't need to perform a version of yourself to be worthy. You don't have to love what others love to belong. Your legacy is built in small, unseen choices like having the courage to say *no* to what no longer feeds you, and the strength to stop performing and start becoming. You are not here to fit someone else's mold. You are here to create something more genuine.

Cauliflower has never just been a vegetable. It used to symbolize everything you were told to like, be, *and* try for acceptance. But just because it's on everyone's plate doesn't mean it belongs on yours. Just because it's praised doesn't mean it's right for you. Just because you're used to having it there doesn't mean it still belongs.

This book is your permission to let go of what no longer serves you. To identify what doesn't fit. To stop trying to reshape yourself to match what was never meant for your growth. Because growth isn't always about blooming; sometimes it's about uprooting. Sometimes it's about choosing a different garden. Sometimes it's about saying, "this isn't for me," and letting that truth be enough. You were never the problem. You were simply trying to thrive in soil that asked you to shrink, silence, or soften yourself into someone more digestible. But your life, your leadership, your legacy, it was never meant to be dull or disguised. It was meant to be yours. And sometimes, all it takes to start anew is a shift in perspective. Looking through your own lens might reveal that the space you once thought wasn't for you can, in fact, be a place where you grow, if you're allowed to show up as yourself. That kind of clarity doesn't just change how you lead. It changes where and why you choose to lead. And that begins the moment you stop forcing yourself to like cauliflower. Because once you stop performing and start becoming, you reclaim the power to choose your impact, not just the position you hold, but the legacy you leave in the lives you touch.

Conclusion

If you have reached this point, pause and take a breath. You have done something many leaders never allow themselves to do. You have reflected deeply on who you are, how you lead, and who you are becoming. That is not a small accomplishment. It is a deliberate act of leadership, one that deserves acknowledgment.

As you reflect on the time you have spent here, I invite you to sit with whatever emotions it stirred. Were there moments that made you uncomfortable? Did certain truths frustrate you or provoke resistance, even anger? Return to those sections. Those reactions are not incidental. They are signals pointing toward places within you that are asking for more honesty, more attention, and more growth. Notice what surfaced as you read. Curiosity. Sadness. Hope. Defensiveness. Let all of it speak. Leadership is not only an intellectual pursuit. It is an emotional one. The more willing you are to engage with those internal responses, the more grounded and effective your leadership becomes.

This work was never about simply reading pages or gathering insight. It was about participation. About honoring the discomfort you were willing to face, the questions you allowed yourself to ask, and the truths you let rise to the surface. You chose engagement over performance. You chose self-examination over avoidance. That choice matters.

Your willingness to move beyond performance and toward authenticity has real impact. It affects the people you lead, the cultures you help shape, and the environments you influence every day. Most importantly, it affects you. Leadership rooted in self-awareness and intention does more than deliver outcomes. It shapes experiences. It changes how people feel in your presence and how they carry that experience forward.

As you return to your work, your teams, your meetings, and your decisions, carry these ideas with you. Let them live in your conversations, your choices, and your presence. You will not always get it right, and that is not a failure. Authentic leadership is not about perfection. It is about alignment. It is about showing up honestly, participating fully, and continually returning to what reflects your values.

Before you close this book, take one more step. Create your leadership compass. This is not a symbolic exercise. It is a practical necessity for leading with clarity and integrity. Your compass is grounded in what you value most, the principles that guide you when pressure is high and clarity feels scarce.

Ask yourself honestly. What do I stand for? What values will I refuse to compromise, regardless of circumstance? What are my deal breakers? These are not preferences. They are boundaries. They protect your leadership from becoming reactive, scattered, or performative. Defining your deal breakers is one of the most important acts of leadership you can undertake because it shifts you from responding to everything to leading from what truly matters.

When you understand where you stand, the weight of leadership becomes more manageable. Decision-making under pressure becomes clearer because you recognize that not every issue requires your energy, defense, or emotional investment. I once had a leader in public education say to me, "Bobbi, you are going to have to decide which hill you are willing to die on. You cannot die on all of them." That guidance shaped how I lead. It taught me that discernment is as essential as decisiveness.

Here is the power of knowing your deal breakers. Once they are defined, everything else becomes open to exploration. This is where opportunity emerges. With your non-negotiables protected, you can approach challenges with curiosity instead of defensiveness and flexibility instead of rigidity. You lead with confidence not because you control every outcome, but because your core is steady. That steadiness invites others to take risks, engage honestly, and grow alongside you.

Your leadership compass is the internal guide that keeps you anchored when circumstances are unpredictable. It allows you to lead with consistency, confidence, and compassion. Not because you have all the answers, but because you know what you will not compromise.

Build it. Write it down. Name your values. Identify your deal breakers. Let them guide your decisions, your conversations, and your presence. Leadership without a compass is reaction. Leadership with a compass is alignment. It is where integrity holds. It is where authentic leadership begins.

Take a moment to acknowledge how far you have come and then continue forward. Keep growing. Keep choosing courage, care, and clarity. The most powerful leadership is never rooted in performance. It is rooted in participation. It is rooted in presence. And your willingness to lead from that place is already evidence of what is possible.

Leadership is like cauliflower. You can dress it up, season it, and present it in ways that appeal to others. But if it does not align with who you truly are, no amount of presentation will make it right. The real work of leadership is not learning to tolerate what does not fit. It is having the courage to know your truth, lead from it unapologetically, and trust that authenticity will always nourish more than performance ever could.

Not everything praised belongs on your plate. Not everything familiar still serves you. This book has never been about forcing yourself to like what was never meant for you. It is permission to let go of what no longer fits. To stop reshaping yourself for acceptance. To recognize that growth is not always about blooming. Sometimes it is about uprooting. Sometimes it is about choosing different soil.

You were never the problem. You were trying to thrive in environments that asked you to shrink, soften, or perform. Your leadership, your life, and your legacy were never meant to be muted or disguised. They were meant to be yours.

When you stop performing and start becoming, you reclaim the power to choose your impact. Not just the position you hold, but the experience you leave behind. And that choice, made quietly and consistently, is what defines a lasting legacy.

www.ingramcontent.com/pod-product-compliance
Lightning Source LLC
LaVergne TN
LVHW010655110826
845149LV00014B/3099

* 9 7 9 8 9 9 4 6 7 2 2 0 4 *